lonely planet

# POCKET

# PHILADELPHIA

TOP SIGHTS • LOCAL EXPERIENCES

SIMON RICHMOND

# Contents

## Plan Your Trip

Benjamin Franklin Bridge (p43)
DARREN LOPRINZI / 500PX ©

## Explore Philadelphia 29

## Survival Guide 147

## Special Features

# Welcome to Philadelphia

Blessed with the glamour and culture of a big city, 'Philly' as it's affectionately known, also delights visitors with its rich history and small-town charm. Easy to explore and embracing of nature, this Unesco World Heritage City has a soul suffused with a passion for life's pleasures including art, food and nightlife.

Schuylkill Banks and Center City JUMPING ROCKS/UIG/GETTY IMAGES ©

# Top Sights

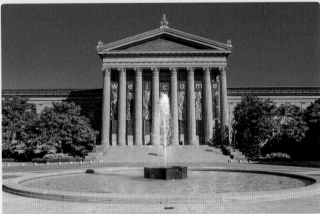

FOTOS593/SHUTTERSTOCK ©

### Philadelphia Museum of Art

Philadelphia's premier artistic storehouse. **p84**

### Reading Terminal Market

Mammoth multiethnic food market. **p54**

SEAN PAVONE/SHUTTERSTOCK ©

## Fairmount Park

The largest urban park in the US. **p90**

## Independence Hall

The birthplace of the US. **p32**

DERVIN WITMER/SHUTTERSTOCK ©

FILIPHOTO/SHUTTERSTOCK ©

## City Hall

The largest municipal building in the US. **p72**

FLIPHOTO/SHUTTERSTOCK ©

FAR LEFT: JON LOVETTE/GETTY IMAGES ©, LEFT: LORI LABRECQUE/SHUTTERSTOCK ©

### Barnes Foundation

Visual feast of *objects d'art*. **p90**

### Eastern State Penitentiary

Fascinating ruined jail. **p90**

### Philadelphia's Magic Gardens
Mosaic wonderland. **p124**

### South 9th Street Italian Market
Historic market. **p120**

### Museum of the American Revolution
The Revolution brought to life. **p38**

# Eating

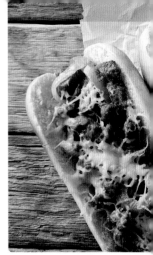

*Philadelphia has an incredibly diverse, vibrant food scene. German and Italian influences are predominant, but these days they're part of a brilliant mix that runs the gamut from Burmese noodles to vegan delights. Whether you're in search of the ideal cheesesteak or a James Beard Award winner, Philly delivers.*

## Where to Eat

The hot restaurant strips are E Passyunk Ave, between Dickinson and McKean Sts in South Philadelphia, and Frankford Ave in Fishtown. You'll also find plenty of choice in Center City, particularly in Midtown Village/the Gayborhood and Chinatown.

For cheap eats, including the legendary Philly cheesesteak (pictured above), South St is a go-to spot. Bargain eats are also a feature of University City, as are food trucks. In fact food trucks are a common sight across the city; Food Truck Nation (www.food trucknation.us) has found Philadelphia to be among the top five friendliest cities in the US for these mobile meal outlets.

## BYOB

Many restaurants have a BYOB – bring your own bottle (of wine or beer) – policy. At most places there's no charge for this, but if there is it's unlikely to be more that a couple of bucks. Another bonus is that the majority of the clientele at these restaurants are usually locals, as people who live in the area are more likely to take the extra step of first going to a wine shop (which are not very common, due to Pennsylvania liquor laws).

## Best Top End Dining

**Vetri Cucina** Elegant, classic Italian food in an intimate Midtown Village town house. (p59)

**Zahav** Golden Israeli-influenced gastronomy from award-winning chef Michael Solomonov. (p45)

**Morimoto** Iron Chef Morimoto's establishment is as extravagant as the show. Plan on being wowed at every bite. (p60)

AS FOOD STUDIO/SHUTTERSTOCK ©

## Best Budget Dining

**Reading Terminal Market** Eat everything from Pennsylvania Dutch treats to Thai curry. (p54)

**Frieda** Superior cafe with home-baked treats and a packed schedule of events. (p51)

**Hardena/Waroeng Surabaya** James Beard–nominated Indonesian cafe where the rice plates can't be beat. (p126)

**Rooster Soup Co** Smoked matzo-ball soup and other diner delights. (p75)

## Best Cheesesteaks & Sandwiches

**Pat's King of Steaks** Invented the cheesesteak, way back in 1930. (p130)

**Joe's Steaks & Soda Shop** Fishtown hub for cheesesteaks, including a vegan version. (p109)

**John's Roast Pork** Classic, cash-only joint in business since 1930. (p129)

## Best Vegetarian & Vegan

**Vedge** Vegan fine-dining that will sweep you away with its finesse. (p60)

**V Street** Street food so good that you'll not miss the lack of meat. (p74)

### Foodie Websites

**Foobooz** (www.phillymag.com/foobooz) Current dining scene news and listings.

**Eater Philadelphia** (https://philly.eater.com) News and reviews on where to eat.

# History & Culture

*Philadelphia's prominence in US history is a source of great civic pride. The 17th-century creation of idealistic English Quaker William Penn, the city's name comes from ancient Greek and means 'brotherly love.' A past state and national capital, Philly was where the colonies declared their Independence.*

EQROY/SHUTTERSTOCK ©

## World Heritage City

Declared a World Heritage City by Unesco in 2015, Philadelphia cherishes and protects its earliest days within the Independence National Historical Park of the Old City. Visiting original institutions such as Independence Hall and seeing iconic landmarks like the Liberty Bell will help you appreciate the deep passion for freedom that motivated the new nation's founders. Excellent museums devoted to the Constitution, the American Revolution and Benjamin Franklin round out that education.

## Multicultural Philly

By any measure Philadelphia is a diverse city. Its population breaks down into roughly 44% black, 35% white, 14% Latino or Hispanic and 7% Asian and other races. Search out the museums and locations that celebrate the contributions and achievements of this rich multiethnic population. Then go that bit deeper into the more eclectic and specialised corners of Philly's past at the fascinating Mütter Museum with its collection of medical oddities or the Wagner Free Institute of Science, which is home to an extraordinary natural-history collection unchanged since the 1890s.

## Best History Museums

**Museum of the American Revolution** Exhibition bringing the birth of the nation spectacularly to life. (pictured above; p38)

**National Constitution Center** Many interactive exhibits plus a live performance on the evolution of

RITU MANOJ JETHANI/SHUTTERSTOCK ©

the Constitution. (pictured above; p38)

**Philadelphia History Museum at the Atwater Kent** Exhibitions on the city's richly endowed past. (p41)

**National Museum of American Jewish History** Detailed exhibitions illuminate the role of Jewish culture in the US. (p39)

## Best African American History

**African American Museum in Philadelphia** Learn about trailblazing activists. (p58)

**Johnson House** See where fleeing slaves were hidden in this Germantown home. (p117)

**Mother Bethel AME Church** Birthplace of the African Methodist Episcopal Church. (p40)

**President's House Site** Learn about the lives of the slaves who were part of George Washington's household. (p42)

## Best House Museums

**Physick House** Society Hill house of the 'Father of American Surgery,' with attractively furnished rooms. (p41)

**Rosenbach Museum & Library** Tour this storied literary library in a beautiful town house. (p72)

**Historic Strawberry Mansion** The largest historic property in Fairmount Park houses some fine antiques. (p87)

# Drinking & Nightlife

*Whether you're in search of a beer, a cocktail or a cup of joe, Philly delivers. The Old City boasts the highest concentration of liquor licenses in the US after New Orleans. Craft brewing is big here, while artisan spirits distilling is also on the rise, with several distilleries open for tours and tastings on the weekends.*

RICHARD T. NOWITZ/GETTY IMAGES ©

## Best Bars

**Trestle Inn** Who doesn't love a cool cocktail bar with a glitter ball, DJs and go-go girls? (p110)

**Charlie Was a Sinner** Heavenly vegan cocktails at this Midtown Village charmer. (p62)

**Bob & Barbara's Lounge** Classic low-frills, cheap drinks boozer with drag shows, live jazz, karaoke and more. (p78)

## Best Coffee & Tea

**La Colombe Fishtown** Premium coffee and artisan spirits, including creamy lattes. (p111)

**The Random Tea Room** Pure pleasure for tea fans with some 40 blends to choose from. (p111)

**Elixir Coffee Roasters** Quality hand-dripped coffee at this alleyway cafe in Center City. (p69)

## Best Craft Beer & Spirits

**Monk's Cafe** Offers an incredible selection of ales from across the world. (p76)

**Yards Brewing Company** Huge new drinking and dining facility for this well-established brewer. (pictured above; p112)

**Philadelphia Distilling** Tour the distillery and get merry on its gin and absinthe cocktails. (p112)

**Second District Brewing** Craft brews in an off-the-radar section of South Philly. (p130)

# Shopping

ROBERT K. CHIN · STOREFRONTS/ALAMY STOCK PHOTO ©

*There are plenty of interesting options, from authentic Italian groceries to arty souvenirs. Browse the racks in one of America's grandest and oldest department stores or go food shopping in one of the country's best indoor markets. With no sales tax on clothing it's also the place to invest in an upgrade or refresh of your wardrobe.*

## Where to Shop

Center City is where most of the shopping action is to be found with Rittenhouse Row (www.rittenhouserow. org) styling itself as the premier retail area, packed with national and international brand stores. Serious competition will come from the new mega-mall Fashion District, spanning three blocks along Market St in Center City East.

For arts, crafts and quirky boutiques zone in on N 2nd and N 3rd Sts in Old City.

The east end of South St is also good retail hub, packing plenty of boho-style.

## Best for Food & Drink

**Reading Terminal Market** Not-to-be-missed gourmet shopping destination with oodles of edible souvenirs. (p54)

**South 9th Street Italian Market** A thrilling retail option for the culinary minded. (p120)

**Shane Confectionery** Willy Wonka's dream sweet shop creates old-fashioned, delicious candies and chocolates. (pictured above; p48)

**Art in the Age** Inspiring range of goods for both casual cocktail makers and serious mixologists. (p49)

## Best for Fashion

**Boyd's** Style and superb service at this elegant throwback to the glory days of fashion retail. (p80)

**Meadowsweet Mercantile** Vintage apparel is given a chic makeover here. (p51)

**Lapstone & Hammer** An old wedding-dress shop houses this excellent men's fashion boutique. (p65)

**Joan Shepp** Stylish female boutique stocking some of the classiest global labels. (p81)

# Architecture

MISHELLA/SHUTTERSTOCK ©

*Imaginative architecture has long been part of Philadelphia's DNA. The city doubles as an open-air museum with contributions from almost all periods of American architecture and important buildings by key talents including William Strickland, Frank Furness, Louis Kahn, IM Pei and Norman Foster.*

## Skyscrapers

Center City began to reach for the skies in the 1980s when One Liberty Place began construction. Among more recent contributions to the city's skyline are the 58-story, 975ft Comcast Center; and Norman Foster's Comcast Innovation & Technology Center, Philly's tallest building.

## Row Houses

Not for nothing did Philadelphia become known as the 'City of Homes'. Row houses are emblematic of the city's streetscapes. You'll notice three distinct types: old individual and double houses, such as those found in Old City and Society Hill; the monumental rows of mansion houses that are prominent around Rittenhouse and Fitler Sq; and, as you move to the city's edges, the smaller, simpler and – crucially – more affordable late-19th- and early-20th-century row houses built for workers.

## Best Architecture

**City Hall** Spectacular building topped by giant statue of William Penn. (pictured above; p72)

**30th St Station** Grand 1930 railway terminus with awe-inspiring interior. (p139)

**Anne & Jerome Fisher Fine Arts Building** One of the finest remaining works by Frank Furness. (p139)

**Parkway Central Library** Join one of the free architectural tours around this splendid public building. (p91)

**Rodeph Shalom Synagogue** Spectacular decorations both inside and out. (p106)

# Arts & Crafts

*Philadelphia's rich and varied arts scene has deep roots. The city is home to the oldest art school and museum in the US and is where the 18th-century portraitist Charles Wilson Peale, the painter Thomas Eakins and the sculptor Alexander Milne Calder all practiced their crafts.*

4KCLIPS/SHUTTERSTOCK ©

## Public Art

One of the reasons Philadelphia has so much public art is that since 1959 the city has pioneered the Percent for Art model requiring the inclusion of site-specific public art in new constructions or major renovation projects.

Contemporary artists are well represented across the city, not least in the thousands of pieces of street art created as part of the hugely successful Mural Arts Program. You also won't be able to miss the distinctive mosaic mural art of Isaiah Zagar, which is especially prevalent on the streets of South Philadelphia where the artist has been based for over 50 years.

## Best Art Galleries

**Philadelphia Museum of Art** The big one, a storehouse of art from throughout the ages. (pictured above; p84)

**Barnes Foundation** Some 180 Renoirs and much more in this fabulous art collection. (p90)

**Pennsylvania Academy of the Fine Arts** In an astonishing building designed by Frank Furness and George Hewitt. (p72)

**Institute of Contemporary Art** The art zeitgeist where Andy Warhol had his first major show. (p139)

**Fabric Workshop & Museum** Admire material creations by top artists. (p58)

## Best Crafts

**Philadelphia's Magic Gardens** Hands-on creativity activities can be added on to the tours here. (p124)

**Expressive Hand** BYOB to aid creativity at this hands-on pottery painting studio. (p131)

**Clay Studio** Pottery classes are held at this Old City gallery and shop. (p35)

# Entertainment

*Philadelphia's culture scene hums, both with homegrown talent and great touring acts. For classical music and ballet, ticket prices are low compared with NYC; likewise, you could see a great rock show for $10. There's plenty of free entertainment, too, including superb classical music recitals.*

JEROME LABOUYRIE/SHUTTERSTOCK ©

## Live Music

Philly's indie rock scene is the envy of other American metropolises. A key player is R5 Productions (www.r5productions.com). Its primary aim is to put on rock shows 'for the kids, by the kids', which translates into good-quality bands and singers in decent venues at affordable prices (ie under $14 a ticket). Many of its regular gigs are open to those under 21; liquor licences at other performance venues means these gigs are always for those 21 and over.

## Best Entertainment

**Kimmel Center** Offers classical music, ballet, Broadway shows and more. (pictured above; p79)

**Mann Center** Summer concerts are held at this superb outdoor arena overlooking the city skyline. (p98)

**Union Transfer** Lofty ceilings provide great acoustics at this live-music venue. (p114)

**Curtis Institute of Music** Attend some extraordinary recitals, many of them free. (p79)

**Johnny Brenda's** Fishtown venue that's a touchstone of Philly's indie-rock scene. (p114)

## Online Resources

**Uwishunu** (www.uwishunu.com) Regularly updated listings on events.

**Philadelphia Weekly** (www.philadelphiaweekly.com) Weekly updated listings.

# Green Spaces

*Greenery softens Philly's streets and avenues. William Penn's original town plan included five park squares. Covering over 2000 acres Fairmount Park is the nation's largest urban park and over three times the size of New York's Central Park. The bicycle and jogging paths of the Schuylkill River Trails are also prime urban resources.*

JON LOVETTE/GETTY IMAGES ©

## Rail Park

The first phase of the Rail Park (p106) is now open. This is a major milestone in a plan first advocated in 2003 as an imaginative way to reuse 3 milles of decommissioned rail lines between Fairmount Park and Center City. When fully completed, the park will be twice the length and width of New York City's High Line Park, with dedicated cycle paths and performance spaces in the vaulted tunnels.

## Best Parks

**Fairmount Park** The largest city park in the US is bisected by the Schuylkill River. (p90)

**Schuylkill Banks** Cycling and jogging trails, as well as yoga, kayaking and boat tours in warmer weather. (p73)

**Wissahickon Valley Park** It's hard to believe this densely wooded park is within the city limits. (pictured above; p96)

**FDR Park** A 340-acre recreation space in South Philly popular with skateboarders, joggers and picnickers. (p125)

**Clark Park** Home to a rare public statue of Charles Dickens as well as a weekly farmers market. (p142)

**Spruce St Harbor Park** Swing in a hammock at this seasonal park on the Delaware. (p35)

## Best Gardens & Squares

**Shofuso Japanese House & Garden** Admire the manicured horticulture of this garden in West Fairmount Park. (p93)

**Bartram's Garden** National Historic Landmark garden dating back to 1728. (p145)

**Rittenhouse Sq** Prestigious urban square planted with lofty trees and with a central fountain. (p74)

# For Kids

*Whatever age your kids are, Philadelphia is a very child-friendly city with tons of things to see and do as a family. Museums and galleries go out of their way to appeal to children while the city's many parks and outdoor spaces are perfect for playgrounds. A great resource is Mommy Poppins (https://mommypoppins.com).*

MIRA/ALAMY STOCK PHOTO ©

## Best Kid-Friendly Museums

**Franklin Institute** The reigning champion of interactive displays. Walk through a giant heart, ride a steam train, watch an IMAX movie. (p91)

**Please Touch Museum** Giant toys allow kids to learn through play. (pictured above; p92)

**Academy of Natural Sciences** Brave the dinosaurs, a roomful of live butterflies and dig for a fossil. (p93)

**Independence Seaport Museum** Everything you'd care to learn about the marine environment and boats, plus a historic US battleship and submarine to explore. (p35)

## Best Playgrounds & Animal Encounters

**Smith Memorial Playground** Historic playground and playhouse freely open to kids aged 10 or younger. (p97)

**Philadelphia Zoo** Home to nearly 1300 animals, including tigers and polar bears, housed in naturalistic habitats. (p94)

**Adventure Aquarium** One of the largest aquariums in the US is across the Delaware in Camden. (p44)

**Franklin Square** Part of William Penn's town plan, this square includes a carousel and a mini-golf course. (p44)

## Best Teen Attractions

**Eastern State Penitentiary** The audio tour around this crumbling and spooky old jail is packed with fascinating tales. (p90)

**Mütter Museum** Older kids will love the collection of 139 human skulls and the saponified body of the 'Soap Lady'. (p72)

**Paine's Park** Bring a skateboard and practice some tricks at this dedicated skatepark beside the Schuylkill River. (p94)

# LGBT+

EQROY/SHUTTERSTOCK ©

*Wherever you fall on the gender/sexuality spectrum, Philly will open its arms to you. In 1965 Independence Hall was the site of one of the first gay-rights protests in US history. The 'Gayborhood' (pictured right) may have been rebranded Midtown Village, but you'll still see plenty of rainbow flags and LGBT-friendly bars and business here.*

## Support Center

A cornerstone of the Gayborhood is the dynamic **William Way LGBT Community Center** (☏215-732-2220; www.waygay.org; 1315 Spruce St, Midtown Village; ⏰11am-10pm Mon-Fri, noon-5pm Sat & Sun; ⓢWalnut-Locust). As well as providing support it hosts a wide range of events and activities – from art shows and music festivals to skills classes – many of them free. On the side of the building look for the LGBT+ history mural *Pride and Progress*.

## LGBT+ Events

The LGBT+ film festival **qFLIX** (www.qflixphilly.com; ⏰Mar) has screenings on a variety of queer themes.

**Philadelphia Black Pride** (www.phillyblackpride.org; ⏰Apr) aims to transform the lives of LGBT+ people of color.

The **Philly Dyke March** (www.facebook.com/philadelphiadykemarch) through the city center is held in early June a day before **Philly Pride** (www.phillygaypride.org; ⏰Jun).

## Best for LGBT+ Travelers

**Woody's** Anchor bar of the Gayborhood. (p64)

**Tavern on Camac** A piano bar downstairs and DJs upstairs. (p64)

**Toasted Walnut Bar & Kitchen** Newer venue that caters primarily for women into women. (p64)

**Voyeur** For dancing until near dawn, this after-hours club is your option. (p64)

**Philly AIDS Thrift @ Giovanni's Room** LGBT+ reads, often holds author talks on the weekends. (p65)

# Four Perfect Days

## Day 1

Go early to the **Independence Visitor Center** (p153) to secure a timed ticket to visit **Independence Hall** (p32). Learn about the important principles behind the founding of the US at the **National Constitution Center** (p38) and the **Liberty Bell Center** (p38).

After lunch at **High Street on Market** (p45) get some more historical background at the **Museum of the American Revolution** (p38). Explore **Elfreth's Alley** (p35) and the boutiques and art galleries of the Old Town, dropping into **Shane Confectionery** (p48) for some sweet treats.

Enjoy modern Israeli food at **Zahav** (p45), then move on to **Tattooed Mom** (p130) for a cocktail or two.

## Day 2

Breakfast at **Reading Terminal Market** (p54), then view the eye-popping interiors of the **Masonic Temple** (p58) or the impressive **Pennsylvania Academy of the Fine Arts** (p72).

Dine for a good cause at **Rooster Soup Co** (p75) before or after the 12:30pm tour of **City Hall** (p72), which includes the chance to stand directly beneath the giant statue of William Penn. Snap a selfie in front of the LOVE sculpture in **JFK Plaza** (p69).

Sup on vegan street food at **V Street** (p74). Enjoy a craft beer at **Monk's Cafe** (p76) or catch a free performance by the supremely talented students at the **Curtis Institute of Music** (p79).

## Day 3

SCOTT VRANA/500PX ©

Stroll through **Fairmount Park** (p90) before dipping into the amazing collection at the **Philadelphia Museum of Art** (p84). Squeeze in the nearby **Rodin Museum** (p92) before lunch at **Whole Foods Market** (p95).

Spend the afternoon browsing Cezannes, Renoirs and Picassos at the **Barnes Foundation** (p90) or take a tour around the fascinating **Eastern State Penitentiary** (p90).

Stretch your legs at the **Rail Park** (p106). Down a pint at **Yards Brewing Company** (p112) followed by superb noodles at **Stock** (p107). Enjoy live music at **Johnny Brenda's** (p114) or boogie with go-go dancers at the **Trestle Inn** (p110).

## Day 4

SUSAN E DEGGINGER/ALAMY STOCK PHOTO ©

Explore the **South 9th Street Italian Market** (p120), then be blown away by Isaiah Zagar's mosaic art masterpiece **Philadelphia's Magic Gardens** (p124).

Head over to University City for lunch at **White Dog Cafe** (p139). Stroll around the U Penn campus, dropping into **Penn Museum** (p141) and the beautiful **Anne & Jerome Fisher Fine Arts Building** (p139). Also check out what's showing at the **Institute of Contemporary Art** (p139).

See a performance at the **Kimmel Center** (p79) or **Academy of Music** (p79), then hit Midtown Village, aka the Gayborhood, for fun times at bars such as **Woody's** (p64) and **Dirty Franks** (p61).

# Need to Know

For detailed information, see Survival Guide (p147)

**Population**
1.57 million

**Currency**
US Dollar ($)

**Money**
ATMs widely available; credit cards accepted at most places. Some restaurants and bars are cash-only.

**Language**
English

**Time**
Eastern Standard/ Daylight Time (GMT/ UTC minus five/four hours)

**Visas**
The US Visa Waiver Program allows nationals of 38 countries to enter the US without a visa.

**Phones**
Most US mobile (cell) phones besides the iPhone operate on CDMA, not the European standard GSM. Check compatibility with your phone service provider.

## Daily Budget

### Budget: Less than $150

Dorm bed: $20–30

Sightseeing/admission fees: $40

Cheesesteak: $9

Three slices of pizza: $12

Pabst Blue Ribbon and a shot: $3

PHLASH bus day ticket: $5

### Midrange: $150–250

Double room in a hotel: $120

Sightseeing/admission fees: $40

Lunch at a chic cafe: $20

Dinner without alcohol: $40–50

### Top end: More than $250

Chic hotel room: $200–400

Sightseeing/admission fees: $60

Lunch with alcohol: $35

Dinner with alcohol: $60–100

Two cocktails: $30

## Advance Planning

**Two months before** Book hotel reservations as soon as possible – prices increase the closer you get to your arrival date.

**Three weeks before** If you haven't done so already, score a table at your top-choice high-end restaurant.

**One week before** Surf the web and scan blogs and Twitter for the latest restaurant and bar openings, plus upcoming art exhibitions.

# Arriving in Philadelphia

### ✈ Philadelphia International Airport

The Airport Line train ($6.75, 25 minutes, every 30 minutes) stops at University City and Center City. A taxi to the center costs a flat fare of $28.50.

### 🚆 30th St Station

The Market-Frankford subway line, Trolley lines and Regional Rail Lines can get you to many places around the city. Buses and taxis are also plentiful.

### 🚆 Greyhound Terminal

From the terminal you're within walking distance of most of the Center City. Access the subway at 11th St or Regional Rail lines at Jefferson Station.

# Getting Around

For timetables and further information check with **SEPTA** (☎215-580-7800; www.septa.org), which runs Philadelphia's transit system.

### 🚶 Walking

Downtown you can walk between most places easily.

### Ⓢ Subway & Trolley

Philly has two subways and a trolley line (fare $2.50). Purchase the stored-value key card for discounted fares.

### 🚌 Buses

Convenient for quick hops across Center City and further afield.

### 🚕 Taxi

Easy to hail Downtown. Flag fall is $2.70, then $2.30 per mile or portion thereof. Uber and Lyft are also commonly used.

# Philadelphia Neighborhoods

### Logan Square & Fairmount (p83)
Head here to visit the Philadelphia Museum of Art and several other key museums. Fairmount Park stretches northwest to the Falls Bridge near Manayunk and is divided by the Schuylkill River.

◉
*Philadelphia Museum of Art*

### University City & West Philadelphia (p137)
West of the Schuylkill River is the Ivy League University of Pennsylvania. The campus makes for a pleasant afternoon stroll and has an excellent museum and library.

### Rittenhouse Square & Center City West (p67)
Center City is dominated by office buildings, big hotels and restaurants. Genteel Rittenhouse Sq is a quiet counterpoint, while the area's western edge is fringed by the Schuylkill Banks park.

### Fishtown & Northern Liberties (p103)

These areas north of Rte 30 and east of Broad St are increasingly popular spots to eat, drink, party and shop. Many craft beer and spirits producers are based here.

**Reading Terminal Market** ◉

**Independence Hall** ◉

**South 9th Street Italian Market** ◉

### Chinatown & Center City East (p53)

Come here for the historic Reading Terminal Market and the US's fourth-largest Chinatown. LGBT+ visitors will feel at home in the 'Gayborhood,' also known as Midtown Village.

### South Philadelphia (p119)

This sprawling, multicultural district stretches down to the south end of Broad St where you'll find the repurposed Navy Yards, FDR Park and the city's major sports stadiums.

### Old City & Society Hill (p31)

These districts include a national park protecting historic buildings, the riverfront of Penn's Landing and one of Philly's most stylish residential neighborhoods.

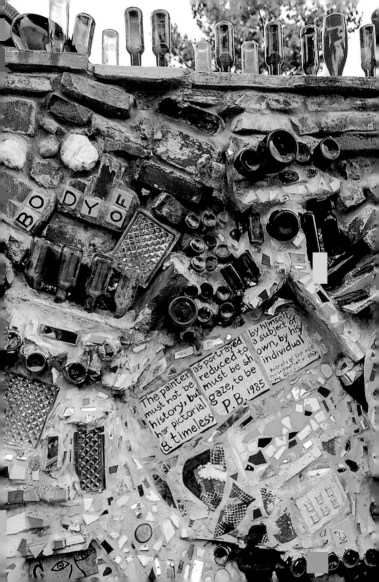

BO DY OF

The painter as portrayed by himself,
must not be reduced to a subject of
history, but must be shown, by his
her pictorial gaze, to be
& timeless P.B. 1985 individual

# Explore
# Philadelphia

Philadelphia's Magic Gardens (p124) STEFANIE METZGER/SHUTTERSTOCK ©

# Explore ⊚
# Old City
# & Society Hill

*The United States founding is writ large across the Old City, a large L-shaped chunk of which is a national park. Across the sunken Delaware Expwy (I-95) the old wharves are now the various public facilities and parks of Penn's Landing. South of Walnut St, largely residential Society Hill is one of Philadelphia's most stylish neighborhoods.*

*Set aside a day to fully experience the Independence National Historical Park as well as photogenic spots such as Elfreth's Alley (p35) and the Dream Garden (p40) mosaic. A walking tour is a great way to get a feel for the area, and if you're in the mood for really stretching your legs there are spectacular views from the footpath over the Benjamin Franklin Bridge (p43). Society Hill is a pleasant, noncommercial area with a handful of attractive historic buildings, while a stroll along Penn's Landing is also recommended, particularly in the summer when Spruce St Harbor Park (p35) is open.*

## Getting There & Around

🚌 Use SEPTA buses or catch the PHLASH bus along Market and Walnut Sts.

⛴ From late May to early September the RiverLink shuttles between Penn's Landing and Camden's waterfront every 30 minutes.

Ⓢ Hop on or off the Market-Frankford Line subway at 5th or 2nd St stations.

## Neighborhood Map on p36

Elfreth's Alley (p35) JAMEGAW/SHUTTERSTOCK ©

Top Sight 📷

# Independence Hall

*It was in this beautifully balanced Georgian building that the Second Continental Congress met to hammer out the Declaration of Independence in 1776, as well as other key foundation documents, including the Constitution. Entry to this World Heritage Site, which started life in 1756 as the Pennsylvania State House, is by tour only.*

◎ MAP P36, B5

📞 877-444-6777

www.nps.gov/inde

520 Chestnut St, Old City

admission free

🕘 9am-5pm, to 7pm late May–early Sep

Ⓢ 5th St

## Supreme Court Chamber

To your right as you enter, this room has been restored using the colors that would have been used in the 18th century and around 70% of the woodwork is original. The Pennsylvania coat of arms, dating from 1785, hangs over the judge's chair. It replaced King George III's coat of arms, which was burned outside in Penn Sq (the location of today's City Hall) on July 8, 1776, the day the Declaration of Independence was read in public for the first time. The furniture you see here and elsewhere in the building are not the originals – those pieces were used for firewood by British troops when they occupied Philadelphia from 1777 to '78 during the War for Independence.

## Assembly Room

Across the hall, the Assembly Room (pictured left) is where most of the building's notable events took place. Delegates from the 13 colonies met here to approve the Declaration of Independence (July 4, 1776) and the design of the US flag (1777). It was here, too, that the Articles of Confederation (1781) were drafted and the US Constitution (1787) produced. Center stage is the chair carved with a rising sun motif that George Washington sat in during the Constitutional Convention. Following his assassination, President Abraham Lincoln lay in state here for two days from April 22, 1865.

## West Wing

Leaving the main hall, the separate West Wing houses the Great Essentials Exhibit, where you can see original printed copies of the Declaration of Independence, the Articles of Confederation and the US Constitution. No ticket is necessary to visit here.

### ★ Top Tips

○ You don't need a ticket for the hall if you visit after 5pm during the longer summer opening hours.

○ Arrive at the security screening area in the east wing of Independence Hall approximately 30 minutes prior to the time on your timed entry ticket.

### ✗ Take a Break

Hand-pour single-origin coffee is served at **Menagerie Coffee** (www.menageriecoffee.com; 18 S 3rd St, Old City; ☉7am-7pm Mon-Fri, 8am-7pm Sat & Sun; 🛜; Ⓢ 2nd St), which offers an attractive, chilled space.

Tasty pizza by the slice is found at **Gianfranco Pizza Rustica** (☎215-592-0048; www.gianfranco-pizza.com; 6 N 3rd St, Old City; pizza $10-18; ☉10am-10pm Mon-Thu & Sat, to 11pm Fri; Ⓢ 2nd St), a tiny, bare-bones pie shop with a few seats should you choose to eat in

# Walking Tour 🥾

# **Exploring Old City & Penn's Landing**

*Although dominated by the Independence National Historical Park, Old City isn't only about the events that happened centuries ago: there are contemporary art galleries and shops stocking artisan products here. Take a stroll beside the Delaware River at Penn's Landing, where you'll find several interesting attractions including a summer-season park.*

## **Walk Facts**

**Start** Center for Art in Wood; **S** 2nd St station

**End** Spruce St Harbor Park; **S** 2nd St station

**Length** 1.5 miles; one hour

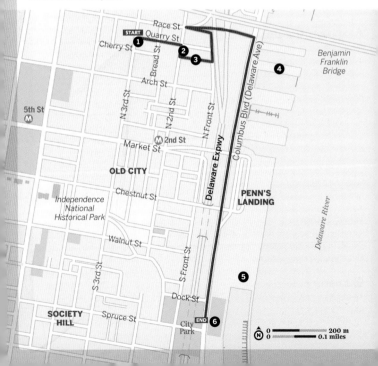

## ❶ Center for Art in Wood

Admire lathe-turned bowls, marquetry, nature photography and timber sculptures at the **Center for Art in Wood** (☎215-923-8000; www.centerforartinwood.org; 141 N 3rd St, Old City; admission free; ⏱10am-5pm Tue-Sat). The gallery here holds several exhibitions a year, there's a museum collection of over a thousand objects and a shop selling handcrafted pieces.

## ❷ Clay Studio

Swing by **Clay Studio's** (☎215-925-3453; www.theclaystudio.org; 139 N 2nd St, Old City; ⏱11am-6pm Mon-Sat, noon-6pm Sun) excellent gallery with regularly changing exhibitions and a cool shop stocking unique one-off items, including mugs and bowls, made by craftspeople from across the US.

## ❸ Elfreth's Alley

Lined with brightly-painted brick row houses fluttering with flags, photogenic cobblestone **Elfreth's Alley** (☎215-574-0560; www.elfreths alley.org; off 2nd St, btwn Arch & Quarry Sts, Old City; tour $5; ⏱museum house noon-5pm Fri-Sun Apr-Nov) dates back to the 1720s, making it America's oldest residential street. Exploring its narrow courtyards is like stepping back in time.

## ❹ Cherry St Pier

This early 20th century municipal **pier** (☎215-629-3200; www.delaware riverwaterfront.com/places/cherry -street-pier; 121 N Columbus Blvd, Penn's Landing), unoccupied since the 1980s, has been revamped as a mixed-use public space with pop-up market, gardens, events and artists' studios. Within the old pier's shell, converted shipping containers make up the studios and market stalls, and there are plans for a drive-in–style cinema.

## ❺ Independence Seaport Museum

This **museum** (☎215-413-8655; www.phillyseaport.org; 211 S Columbus Blvd, Penn's Landing; adult/child $16/12; ⏱10am-5pm, to 7pm Thu-Sat summer, closed Mon Jan-Mar; 🚌12, 21) offers a broad range of maritime-related exhibits and interactive displays, as well as some very unusual items (check out the massive ship-carpenter's screwdriver). Admission includes entry to the 1944 submarine USS *Becuna* and the distinguished 1892 USS *Olympia,* both moored alongside the main building.

## ❻ Spruce St Harbor Park

This summer-season **park** (☎215-922-2386; www.delawareriverwater front.com; 301 S Columbus Blvd; ⏱end Jun-end Aug) is a great place to hang out by the river during the warmer months. Relax in one of the two-person hammocks, take part in free games such as ping-pong and shuffleboard, or knock back craft beers and local eats from the many stalls.

# Old City & Society Hill

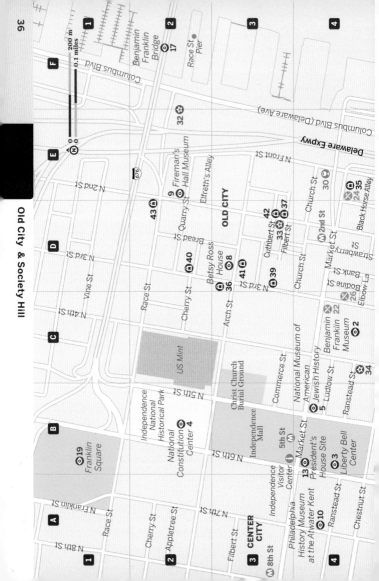

200 m
0.1 miles

Columbus Blvd

Benjamin Franklin Bridge

17

Race St Pier

N 2nd St

676

32

9 Fireman's Hall Museum

Delaware Expwy

Columbus Blvd (Delaware Ave)

N Front St

Efreth's Alley

43

N Quarry St

Bread St

OLD CITY

Cuthbert St

42

33

Filbert St

37

Church St

30

24 35

Black Horse Alley

N 2nd St

Betsy Ross House

40

8

36

41

39

Church St

Market St

Strawberry St

Bank St

Bodine St

Elbow La

26

N 3rd St

N 3rd St

Arch St

Cherry St

Race St

Vine St

Benjamin Franklin Museum

22

2

34

N 4th St

Ranstead St

Ludlow St

5 National Museum of American Jewish History

Commerce St

US Mint

Christ Church Burial Ground

Independence National Historical Park

National Constitution Center 4

19 Franklin Square

N 5th St

Independence Mall

N 6th St

Independence Visitor Center

5th St

Market St

13 President's House Site

3

Liberty Bell Center

N 7th St

Ranstead St

Chestnut St

N Franklin St

Race St

Cherry St

Appletree St

Filbert St

8th St

CENTER CITY

Philadelphia History Museum at the Atwater Kent

10

N 8th St

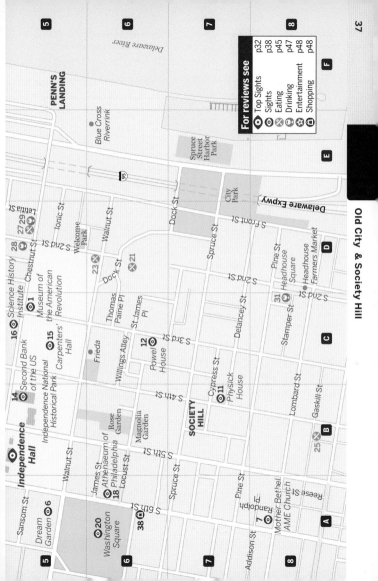

Old City & Society Hill

Delaware River

PENN'S LANDING

Blue Cross Riverrink

**For reviews see**

◉ Top Sights      p32
◉ Sights          p38
⊗ Eating          p45
○ Drinking        p47
✪ Entertainment   p48
⊡ Shopping        p48

Spruce Street Harbor Park

City Park

Delaware Expwy

95

Welcome Park

Lettia St

27 29 ⊗⊗
28
Science History Institute 16 ◉
Chestnut St
S 2nd St
Ionic St

Walnut St

23 ⊗
Dock St
⊗ 21

Spruce St
S Front St

Dock St
S Front St

Museum of the American Revolution ◉ 1

Thomas Paine Pl
St James Pl

Second Bank of the US 14 ◉
Carpenters' Hall ◉ 15
Independence National Historical Park

Frieda

Willings Alley
Powel House ◉ 12
S 3rd St

Pine St
Headhouse Square
S 2nd S
Headhouse Farmers Market
31 ◉
Stamper St
S 2nd S

Delancey St

Physick House ◉ 11
Cypress St
S 4th St

Lombard St
Gaskill St

Independence Hall ◉

Sansom St
Dream Garden ◉ 6

Walnut St
Athenaeum of Philadelphia ◉ 18
Rose Garden
James St
Locust St

Magnolia Garden
S 5th St

SOCIETY HILL

Spruce St

25 ⊗
B

20 ◉
Washington Square
38 ⊡
S 6th St

Pine St
Reese St
Randolph Pl
Mother Bethel AME Church 7 ◉

Addison St

# Sights

## Museum of the American Revolution

MUSEUM

1 ⊙ MAP P36, C5

This impressive, multimedia-rich museum will have you virtually participating in the American Revolution with interactive dioramas and 3D experiences that take you all the way from contentment with British rule to the eventual rejection of it. Learn about the events, people, cultures and religions that participated in one of the world's most important revolutions. Lots of hands-on displays and video stories mean kids will have as much fun as adults. Note that all tickets are timed: reserve them early online. (☎215-253-6731; www. amrevmuseum.org; 101 S 3rd St; adult/student/child $19/17/12; ⊙10am-5pm Sep-late May, 9:30am-6pm late May-Aug; Ⓢ2nd St)

## Benjamin Franklin Museum

MUSEUM

2 ⊙ MAP P36, C4

This underground museum is dedicated to Franklin's storied life as a printer (he started the nation's first newspaper), inventor (bifocals! lightning rods!) and political figure who signed the Declaration of Independence. The exhibition, divided into five areas each focusing on a particular trait of the man, is inventively laid out with interactive elements and plenty of famous Franklin quotations.

In the same courtyard, don't miss the **printing office** (Franklin Court; admission free; ⊙10am-5pm), where park rangers demonstrate an 18th-century printing press similar to that used by Franklin. (☎215-965-2305; www.nps.gov/inde; Market St, btwn 3rd & 4th Sts, Old City; adult/child $5/2; ⊙9am-5pm, to 7pm late May-early Sep; Ⓢ2nd St)

## Liberty Bell Center

HISTORIC SITE

3 ⊙ MAP P36, B4

A glass-walled building protects this icon of Philadelphia history from the elements. You can peek from outside, or join the line to file past, reading about the 2080lb object's history and significance along the way. The line – and it can be a long one in peak summer months – starts on the building's north end.

The gist of the story: originally called the State House Bell, it was made in 1751, to commemorate the 50th anniversary of Pennsylvania's constitution. Mounted in Independence Hall (p32), it tolled on the first public reading of the Declaration of Independence. The crack developed in the 19th century, and the bell was retired in 1846. (☎215-965-2305; www. nps.gov/inde; 526 Market St, Old City; admission free; ⊙9am-5pm, to 7pm late May-early Sep; Ⓢ5th St)

## National Constitution Center

MUSEUM

4 ⊙ MAP P36, B2

This whiz-bang museum makes the US Constitution jump off the page, starting with a dramatic theater-in-the-round presentation by a single actor relating the evolution of the American project. This exits into a dizzying array of interactive exhibits, from voting booths to trivia games. You can also see an original version of the Bill of Rights and be sworn in as president. Go early, both for lighter crowds and a fresher brain – this place is hard to skim through. ( 🕿 215-409-6600; www.constitutioncenter.org; 525 Arch St, Old City; adult/child \$14.50/11; ⏰ 9:30am-5pm Mon-Sat, from noon Sun; 𝐒 5th St)

## National Museum of American Jewish History   MUSEUM

5 ⊚ MAP P36, B4

Covering four floors, with lots of multimedia displays and intrigu-

ing items such as Iriving Berlin's piano and a Yiddish typewriter, this excellent museum is a solid introduction to the history and role of Jewish culture in the US, covering everything from entertainment to the Civil Rights movement.

The ground-floor gift store is a good spot to pick up contemporary and traditional Judaica, including books and decorative religious items such as menorah. ( 🕿 215-923-3811; www.nmajh.org; 101 S Independence Mall E; adult/student/child \$15/13/free; ⏰ 10am-5pm Tue-Fri, to 5:30pm Sat & Sun; 𝐒 5th St)

## Franklin Court   HISTORIC SITE

This peaceful courtyard (see 2 ⊚ Map p36, C4), which can be accessed from both Market and Chestnut St, is where Benjamin Franklin's

Liberty Bell Center

ROMAN BABAKIN/SHUTTERSTOCK ©

Old City & Society Hill Sights

## Storytelling Benches

Between the end of May and early September look for the 13 Storytelling Benches dotted around the Old City. At these spots storytellers enchant listeners young and old with short tales about historical figures and events. Kids can collect a flag and a star from every storyteller on their journey – a full set qualifies for a free carousel ride at Franklin Sq (p44).

home once stood. The house was demolished in 1812 but you can still get a good impression of its dimensions from the tubular steel 3D outline of the building designed by architectural firm Venturi, Rauch, and Scott Brown in 1976. (☎215-965-2305; www.nps.gov; off Market St, btwn 3rd & 4th Sts, Old City; free; ⊙9am-5pm; Ⓢ2nd St)

## Dream Garden          PUBLIC ART

6 ◎ MAP P36, A5

In the east lobby of the Curtis Center is a masterpiece of American craft: a luminous, wall-size Tiffany mosaic of more than 100,000 pieces of glass depicting a lush landscape designed by Maxfield Parrish in 1916.

One of only three such works undertaken by Tiffany Studios, the piece is made up of 24 panels that took six months to install. There's a grand piano in the building lobby that is free for people to play, too.

(☎215-238-6450; 601 Walnut St, Old City; admission free; ⊙8am-6pm Mon-Fri, 10am-1pm Sat; Ⓢ5th St)

## Mother Bethel AME Church          CHURCH

7 ◎ MAP P36, A8

This major historical building is the birthplace of the African Methodist Episcopal (AME) church and is the oldest piece of real estate continually owned by African Americans in the US. The present church, the fourth on the site, dates from 1889 and features gargoyles on its bell tower. The main chapel on the 2nd floor has beautiful stained-glass windows and woodwork.

The original church was founded by two local freed slaves – Richard Allen and Absalom Jones – in 1787. Benjamin Rush, a signer of the Declaration of Independence and among the first white revolutionaries to speak out against slavery, was an initial supporter. It later became a stop on the Underground Railroad when Pastor Allen (entombed in the church) hid hundreds of fugitive slaves prior to the Civil War. There's a small museum in the church dedicated to Allen and a statue of him stands outside. (☎215-925-0616; www.motherbethel. org; 419 St 6th St, Society Hill; admission free; ⊙10am-3pm Tue-Sat, services 8am & 10:45am Sun; 🚌12, 40, 57)

## Betsy Ross House          MUSEUM

8 ◎ MAP P36, D3

Legend has it that this is where America's first flag was made, although most historians doubt it – and it's pretty certain that the actual house Ross lived in was next to this one. Even so, it's a highly popular tourist stop. You get to meet 'Betsy Ross' herself: ask her questions and watch her at work on a flag. (📞215-686-1252; http://historicphiladelphia.org; 239 Arch St, Old City; guided tour adult/child $7/6, self-guided tour adult/child $5/4; 🕙10am-4pm, closed Mon Jan & Feb; 🚇2nd St)

## Fireman's Hall Museum
MUSEUM

**9** 🎯 MAP P36, E2

Learn about everything from fire safety and old fire engines to firefighting techniques and tools at this beautiful museum, housed in a restored 1876 brick fire station. Exhibits include horse-drawn, people-drawn, motorized and steam-powered fire trucks and a recreation of living quarters typical of early professional firefighters.

Note the 'In Memory' plaques on the sidewalk, commemorating firefighters who've died in the line of duty. (📞215-923-1438; www.firemanshallmuseum.org; 147 N 2nd St, Old City; admission free; 🕙10am-4pm Tue-Sat; 🚇2nd St)

## Philadelphia History Museum at the Atwater Kent
MUSEUM

**10** 🎯 MAP P36, A4

Housed in an elegant Greek Revival building designed by John Haviland, this museum houses

several special collections relating to the city's history. On display are paintings by Charles Willson Peale and his sons of local notables, a wampum belt supposedly given to William Penn by the Lenape people and the desk which George Washington used while serving as president in Philadelphia. (📞215-685-4830; www.philadelphiahistory.org; 15 S 7th St, Washington Square West; adult/child $10/free; 🕙10am-4:30pm Tue-Sat; 🚇8th St)

## Physick House
HISTORIC BUILDING

**11** 🎯 MAP P36, B7

Home to the 'Father of American Surgery,' Philip Syng Physick, this stately house has been well preserved. Physick is credited with inventing the stomach pump as well as introducing soda pop to the US, and details of his life are

### Skate Park

From December to March Winterfest sees the **Blue Cross Riverrink** (Map p36, E6; 📞215-925-7465; www.riverrink.com; 101 S Columbus Blvd, Penn's Landing; admission free, skating $3, skate rental $10; 🕙1-11pm Mon-Thu, to 1am Fri, 11am-1pm Sat, 11am-11pm Sun; 🚇2nd St) covered with ice for skating, activities, food stalls, performances and other events, while from Memorial Day to Labor Day Summerfest takes place here with roller-skating.

documented throughout the furnished rooms: look out for the toe-curling illustrations of a lithotomy, an operation to remove gallstones, and the eye-watering implements used for the procedure. (📞215-925-7866; www.philalandmarks.org; 321 S 4th St, Society Hill; $8; ⊙noon-4pm Thu-Sat, from 1pm Sun, by appointment Jan & Feb; 🚌12, 40, 57)

## Powel House
HISTORIC BUILDING

12 ◉ MAP P36, C6

This elegant Georgian brick mansion was home to Samuel Powel, a mayor of Philadelphia in the colonial era, thus a focal point of the city's social life in the 18th century. Noteworthy guests included George and Martha Washington, Benjamin Franklin and John Adams, who enjoyed 'a sinful feast'

here. Its interior is a simulacrum – the original was stripped away decades ago, with parts of it installed in the Philadelphia Museum of Art (p84). (📞215-627-0364; www.philalandmarks.org; 244 S 3rd St, Society Hill; adult/child $8/free; ⊙noon-4pm Thu-Sat, 1-4pm Sun, by appointment Jan & Feb, noon-4pm Wed Memorial Day to Oct; 🚌21, 42, 57)

## President's House Site
HISTORIC SITE

13 ◉ MAP P36, B4

This free outdoor exhibition is constructed on the former location of the presidential offices of George Washington and John Adams. Displays focus on the lives of nine enslaved African Americans who were part of Washington's house-

Interior of Powel House

hold and there's a memorial to all enslaved Africans. It's a powerful reminder of the paradox at the heart of the birth of a free America. (www.phila.gov/presidentshouse; 524–30 Market St, Old City; admission free; ⏱24hr; S 5th St)

## Second Bank of the US
MUSEUM

14 ⊙ MAP P36, B5

Modeled after the Greek Parthenon, this 1824 marble-faced Greek Revival masterpiece now houses a Portrait Gallery. Many of the paintings are by Charles Willson Peale, America's top portrait artist at the time of the American Revolution. (☏215-965-2305; www.nps.gov/inde; 420 Chestnut St, Old City; admission free; ⏱11am-5pm Sat & Sun Mar-Nov, extended hours May-Sep; S 5th St)

## Carpenters' Hall
HISTORIC BUILDING

15 ⊙ MAP P36, C5

Erected as a calling card for the skillful work of the Carpenters' Company of Philadelphia in 1774, this is where the First Continental Congress met. (☏215-925-0167; www.carpentershall.org; 320 Chestnut St, Old City; 10am-4pm Tue-Sun, closed Mon & Tue Jan & Feb; S 5th St)

## Science History Institute
MUSEUM

16 ⊙ MAP P36, C5

A must-stop for scientists and young explorers, this museum offers not just a look back at the history of chemicals and the ma-

terials made from them, but a view into how these products affect our modern lives. Learn about everything from how crayons get their colors to measuring the chemical composition of things in space.

The museum is open until 8pm on the first Friday of each month between March and December. (☏215-925-2222; www.sciencehistory.org; 315 Chestnut St, Old City; admission free; ⏱10am-5pm Tue-Sat; S 5th St)

## Benjamin Franklin Bridge
BRIDGE

17 ⊙ MAP P36, F2

For breathtaking views of the city and Delaware River it's possible to walk or cycle across this 1.8-mile, 800,000-ton suspension bride, which was the longest of its type when it was completed in 1926. Designed by Paul Cret, the bridge connects Philadelphia with Camden, New Jersey, and carries both cars and trains. It is most striking when illuminated at night. (www.drpa.org/bridges/ben-franklin-bridge.html; pedestrian entrance 5th St, Old City; ⏱walkway 6am-8pm Oct-Apr, until 9pm May-Sep; 🚌47, S 5th St or Chinatown)

## Athenaeum of Philadelphia
LIBRARY

18 ⊙ MAP P36, A6

Free exhibitions are held at this special collections library, occupying a National Historic Landmark brownstone building designed in 1845. Curiously, also on display is Napoleon Bonaparte's death mask – part of a collection of

## Camden, New Jersey: The Black Dragon & Other Sights

Noticeably less developed than Philadelphia, Camden – directly across the Delaware River from Penn's Landing – is worth visiting for a couple of attractions and the pleasant waterside park and views. The best of these is the opportunity to tour **Battleship New Jersey** (📞856-966-1652; www.battleshipnewjersey.org; 100 Clinton St; adult/child $21.95/17; ⏱9:30am-3pm; 🚢RiverLink May-Sep, 🚉Broadway/Rand Transportation Center, then NJ Transit's RiverLine to the Entertainment Center), the most decorated such vessel in the US. Nicknamed the 'Black Dragon,' the battleship's guns were able to shoot 23 miles. On Saturday and Sunday at 11am there's a guided 90-minute tour that allows you to see more of the battleship and crawl in a 16-inch gun turret.

Home to over 8500 aquatic creatures from sea turtles to zebra sharks, **Adventure Aquarium** (📞844-474-3474; www.adventure aquarium.com; 1 Riverside Dr; adult/child $29.99/21.99; ⏱9:30am-5pm; 🚢RiverLink May-Sep, 🚉Broadway/Rand Transportation Center, then NJ Transit's RiverLine to the Entertainment Center) is one of the largest such attractions in the US. As well as myriad fish you can also see the 3000lb Nile hippos, Button and Genny, and a flock of African penguins in their own outdoor park.

pieces donated to the Athenaeum by Joseph Bonaparte. Joseph, Napoleon's elder brother, and the former King of Spain, lived in Philadelphia for a while. (📞215-925-2688; www.philaathenaeum.org; 219 S 6th St, Old City; admission free; ⏱9am-5pm Mon-Fri; Ⓢ5th St)

### Franklin Square                          SQUARE

19 ◎ MAP P36, B1

Ringed by busy roads, this square – one of the originals from William Penn's masterplan for his new city – feels somewhat cut off from the other sights of the Old City. Nonetheless, you will find a pretty fountain, a carousel ($3) and a mini-golf course (adult/child $9/7), as well as a seasonal burger shack.

The square has suffered mixed fortunes over the centuries, at one point partially containing a burial ground and at another labelled a Skid Row for drunks. Since its maintenance was contracted out to the non-profit History Philadelphia, and the family-friendly features were added, the square's fortunes have been on the up. A great time to visit is in May and June when the **Chinese Lantern Festival** brightens up the space with 1500 silk lanterns and performances by acrobats and folk dancers. (www.historicphiladelphia. org; Chinatown; Ⓢ5th St)

## Washington Square

SQUARE

**20**  MAP P36, A6

On the northwest edge of Society Hill, this attractive tree-planted square dates back to William Penn's original city plan. In the center is the **Tomb of the Unknown Soldier**, the only monument in the US to both unknown American and British dead of the Revolutionary War.

Back in Penn's day it was called Southeast Sq and was used as a burial ground and pasture. The name was changed in honor of George Washington in 1825 when the land was converted into a formal park. Today it is officially part of the Independence National Historical Park. (www.nps.gov/inde; 9, 21, 47, 5th St)

# Eating

## Zahav

MIDDLE EASTERN $$

**21** MAP P36, D6

Zahav means 'gold' in Hebrew and that's what you'll find here in terms of gastronomy. The menu at this stylish modern Israeli restaurant sees James Beard–award-winning-chef Michael Solomonov drawing primarily from North African, Persian and Levantine kitchens for inspiration.

Pick your own meze and grills, or go for the tasting menu, but under no circumstances bypass their luscious hummus served with a chef's selection of topping. Book well ahead or turn up early (as soon as they open is recommended) for a spot at the bar. (215-625-8800; www.zahavrestaurant.com; 237 St James Pl, Old City; mains $10-14, tasting menus $48; 5-10pm Sun-Thu, to 11pm Fri & Sat; 2nd St)

## High Street on Market

AMERICAN $$

**22** MAP P36, C4

Many Philadelphians swear by High Street's delicious house-made breads and will come here for those alone. They certainly have a creative way with a breakfast or lunch sandwich, salad and soup, too. It's a cozy place, so you're likely to find yourself either sharing a table or waiting a while for a spot. (215-625-0988; https://highstreetonmarket.com; 308 Market St, Old City; mains $10-30; 7am-3:30pm Mon, 7am-3:30pm & 5:30-10pm Tue-Fri, 8am-3:30pm & 5:30-10:30pm Sat, 8am-3:30pm & 5:30-9:30pm Sun; 2nd St)

### Free Yoga

Free yoga classes are held at **Race St Pier** (Map p36, F2; www.delawareriverwaterfront.com; Race St & Delaware Ave, Penn's Landing; 7am-11pm; 2nd St) at 7am and 6pm Monday through Thursday, 7am on Friday, and 9.30am Saturday and Sunday from early April through the first weekend of November.

## Headhouse Farmers Market

The historic Headhouse Shambles, an 18th-century open market hall, comes alive on Sundays with this **farmers' market** (Map p36, D8; http://thefoodtrust.org; cnr 2nd & Lombard Sts, Society Hill; ⏰10am-1pm Sun May-Nov; 🚌12, 40, 57). During the growing season there can be more than 40 produce, snack and craft vendors here.

## City Tavern

AMERICAN $$$

23 🍴 MAP P36, D6

As far as restaurants with costumed waiters go, this is a pretty good one – not too over-the-top and with solid, faintly historical food, such as spicy pepper pot soup. Even if you don't come for a full meal, it's fine to drop by for a drink or snack in its bar. (📞215-413-1443; www.citytavern.com; 138 S 2nd St, Old City; mains $20-36; ⏰11:30am-9pm; Ⓢ2nd St)

## Franklin Fountain

ICE CREAM $

24 🍴 MAP P36, E4

It's cash only at this fantastic yet kitsch-free throwback, from the phosphates and vintage ice-cream flavors (try the teaberry) right down to the ancient telephone and the carton cups. In a nod to modern sensibilities there are vegan ices and treats, too. (📞215-627-1899; www.franklinfountain.com; 116

Market St, Old City; sundaes $10-12; ⏰noon-midnight Mon-Thu, from 11am Fri-Sun; Ⓢ2nd St)

## Marrakesh

MOROCCAN $$

25 🍴 MAP P36, B8

The authentic Moroccan cuisines feast here comprises two appetizers, three main course dishes and two desserts. Plush, patterned carpets, cushions and low tables make a meal here feel like you're dining in the heart of the casbah. (📞215-925-5929; http://marrakesheastcoast.com; 517 S Leithgow St, Washington Sq West; set meal $25; ⏰5:30-10:30pm Sun-Thu, to 11:30pm Fri & Sat; 🚌40, 57)

## Farmicia

AMERICAN $$

26 🍴 MAP P36, C4

Dedicated to simply crafted local and organic foods, the meals here are creative and soul-satisfying. Vegetarians are well-catered for, with a variety of tofu, pasta and veggie-and-grain plates to choose from. There are gluten-free options and weekend brunch rocks, too. (📞215-627-6274; http://farmicia restaurant.com; 15 S 3rd St, Old City; mains $10-29; ⏰11:30am-10pm Tue-Thu, to 11pm Fri, 8:30am-11pm Sat, 8:30am-9pm Sun; 🍴; Ⓢ2nd St)

## Han Dynasty

CHINESE $$

27 🍴 MAP P36, D5

Part of a local mini-empire of sizzling Szechuan goodness. Take your pick from a variety of soups, noodles and spicy entrees. This location has the bonus of a glam dining room in an old bank building. (📞215-922-1888; www.handynasty. net; 123 Chestnut St, Old City; mains $12-21; ⏰11:30am-10pm Sun-Thu, to 10:30pm Fri & Sat; Ⓢ2nd St)

# Drinking

## Khyber Pass Pub
CRAFT BEER

28 🚇 MAP P36, D5

A wide range of craft beers from across the US are sold at this friendly all-day bar. Happy hour runs 4pm to 6pm and the beer menu includes handy tasting notes.

This is also a good-value place to eat. Despite the pub's name, the food is Southern American, featuring dishes such as a beignet (small donuts), shrimp, tasso and grits. (📞215-238-5888; www.khyber

passpub.com; 56 S 2nd St, Old City; ⏰10am-2am; 🛜; Ⓢ2nd St)

## 2nd Story Brewing Co
MICROBREWERY

29 🚇 MAP P36, D5

Brewed on site, 2nd Story's Old City Kölsch, Fritizie's Lager and Declaration IPA are always available alongside at least five other seasonal brews. A flight of four costs $10. (www.2ndstorybrewing. com; 117 Chestnut St, Old City; ⏰11:30am-midnight Sun-Thu, to 2am Fri & Sat; Ⓢ2nd St)

## Panorama
WINE BAR

30 🚇 MAP P36, E4

*The Guinness Book of World Records* has declared Panorama home to the largest wine

Ice cream at Franklin Fountain

preservation and dispensing system in the world (and who are we to argue) with over 150 different wines available either on tap or from the bottle. Flights of five wines are available from $21.75. (📞215-922-7800; www.pennsview hotel.com/panorama; 14 N Front St, Old City; ⏰noon-10pm Mon-Thu, to 11pm Fri, 2-11pm Sat, 5-9pm Sun; 📶; 🚇2nd St)

### Bodhi Coffee                    COFFEE

31 ☕ MAP P36, C8

Something of an alternative neighborhood social scene reigns over this chilled coffee shop, which displays local arts and crafts, and hosts occasional open-mic sessions, book readings and games nights. (📞267-239-2928; www. facebook.com/bodhicoffee; 410 S 2nd St, Society Hill; ⏰7am-6pm Mon-Fri, 8am-6pm Sat & Sun; 🚌40, 57)

# Entertainment

### FringeArts            PERFORMING ARTS

32 ⭐ MAP P36, E2

FringeArts lives up to its name by sticking to its mission of celebrating all that's at the cutting edge (and beyond) of performing arts. Drop by on the first Monday of the month for its Scratch Night, when artists perform samples of new work, or look out for its late-night Get Pegged cabaret. (📞215-413-1318; http://fringearts.com; 140 N Columbus Blvd, Old City; tickets from $5; 🚇2nd St)

### Arden Theatre Co        THEATER

33 ⭐ MAP P36, D3

The musical *Cabaret,* the kid's show *Peter Pan* and Ibsen's *The Dolls House* – the recent offerings by this long-established and well-regarded theater company display its range. There's a 360-seat main stage and 175-seat studio space. (📞215-922-8900; www.ardentheatre. org; 40 N 2nd St, Old City; 🚇2nd St)

### Ritz at the Bourse        CINEMA

34 ⭐ MAP P36, C4

The place to come to see independent and art-house movies as well as special-event screenings such as those offered by National Theatre Live and the Royal Opera House from the UK. Every Friday at midnight they also screen cult movies such as *The Rocky Horror Picture Show*.

Landmark runs a couple more cinemas in the area that show highbrow movies: **Ritz 5** (📞215-440-1184; 214 Walnut St, Old City; 🚇2nd St) and **Ritz East** (📞215-925-4535; 125 S 2nd St, Old City; 🚇2nd St). (📞215-440-1181; www. landmarktheatres.com/philadelphia; 400 Ranstead St, Old City; tickets $8-10.25; 🚇5th St)

# Shopping

### Shane Confectionery        FOOD & DRINKS

35 🛍 MAP P36, E4

Since 1863 this wonderfully old-school candy shop has been

making sweet treats, including buttercreams and slabs, from antique molds. With the shop assistants dressed in Victorian garb it's like stepping back in time. Settle down in the historic hot-chocolate kitchen in the back where you can indulge in a flight of luscious drinks for $12. (📞 215-922-1048; http://shanecandies.com; 110 Market St, Old City; 🕐 9am-9pm Mon & Tue, 11am-8pm Wed & Thu, 11am-10pm Fri & Sat, 11am-9pm Sun; Ⓢ 2nd St)

## Art in the Age    FOOD & DRINKS

36 🔒 MAP P36, D3

Designed as a boutique homage to the cocktail, this spot is both a home-bar supply store and tasting room. Settle down at its bar for a tasting ($7 or $10 depending on your poison) or buy hand-crafted spirits, artisanal bitters and cordials, pickles, long-handled stir spoons, strainers, shakers, recipe books and other cocktail necessities. (📞 215-922-2600; www.artintheage.com; 116 N 3rd St, Old City; 🕐 11am-7pm Mon-Sat, noon-6pm Sun; Ⓢ 2nd St)

## 3rd Street Gallery    ART

37 🔒 MAP P36, D3

Somewhat confusingly, the 3rd Street Gallery is actually located on 2nd St, but that's artists for you – never predictable. They're obviously doing something right here as this artist-run co-op has been going since 1978, making it one of the area's oldest galleries. There are several regularly changing exhibitions on here and they stay open late on First Fridays. (📞 215-625-0993; www.3rdstreetgallery.com;

Shane Confectionery

45 N 2nd St, Old City; ⊘noon-5pm
Wed-Sun; ⓢ2nd St)

## Locks Gallery    ART

**38** 🔒 MAP P36, A6

Exhibitions change every six weeks
or so at this long-running gallery
specializing in contemporary painting and sculpture by both local and
international artists. It occupies a
handsome Italianate Palazzo–style
building, dating from 1918. (📞215-
629-1000; www.locksgallery.com; 600
Washington Sq S, Society Hill; ⊘10am-
6pm Tue-Sat; ⓢ5th St)

## Philadelphia
## Independents    GIFTS & SOUVENIRS

**39** 🔒 MAP P36, D3

The name says it all. Stocking a
wide variety of affordable items by
some 50 local artists and craftspeople, Phi Ind is a go-to destination for original and quirky gifts
and souvenirs, many designed with
a reference to the city. Its range
includes cool t-shirts, jewelry,
accessories, ceramics, prints and
greeting cards. (📞267-773-7316;
www.philadelphiaindependents.com;
35 N 3rd St, Old City; ⊘11am-7pm
Mon-Sat, to 5pm Sun; ⓢ2nd St)

## rennes    FASHION & ACCESSORIES

**40** 🔒 MAP P36, D2

In 2016 this small business making
stylish linen and leather goods
shifted base from Boston to Philly
and hasn't looked back. As well as
its own attractive products, rennes
stocks other designers' fashion
and homewares, including ceramics made from natural materials by

3rd St Gallery (p49)

### Frieda: Eat, Drink, Share & Learn 👍

Not to be missed, **Frieda** (Map p36, C6; ☏ 215-600-1291; http://frieda forgenerations.com; 320 Walnut St, Old City; mains $7.50-13.50; ⊙8am-5pm Tue-Fri, 9am-4:30pm Sat & Sun; 🛜; Ⓢ5th St) aims to connect people of all ages to eat, drink, share and learn something new. It doesn't like to be labeled as one thing or another, but we can assure you it's a great spot for anything from an artisanal tea served with freshly baked cakes and pastries, to a healthy lunch or brunch.

Check online for their monthly schedule of drop-in classes including ones dedicated to drawing, learning a language or how to play games such as mah-jongg. It screen films with discussions afterward and hosts good-value set dinners a couple of times a month.

ethical producers. (☏267-908-4778; www.rennes.us; 135 N 3rd St, Old City; ⊙11am-5pm Tue-Fri, to 6pm Sat, noon-5pm Sun; Ⓢ2nd St)

### Humphry's
GIFTS & SOUVENIRS

**41** 🔒 MAP P36, D3

Looking like an antique version of the United Nations, Humphry's (which was established in 1864) makes flags and banners in all shapes and sizes. If they don't have the flag you need, they'll make it for you. (☏215-922-0510; www.humphrysflag.com; 238 Arch St, Old St; ⊙9am-5pm; Ⓢ2nd St)

### Meadowsweet Mercantile
FASHION & ACCESSORIES

**42** 🔒 MAP P36, D3

Vintage apparel gets a stylish makeover at this appealing boutique full of t-shirts, jeans, sweaters and accessories. Toward the back there's a separate sec-

tion stocking Cuttalossa (www.cuttalossa.us) homewares and linens, as well as local pottery, alpaca socks, teas and beeswax candles. (☏215-756-4802; http://shopatmeadowsweet.com; 47 N 2nd St, Old City; ⊙noon-7pm Mon-Sat, to 5pm Sun; Ⓢ2nd St)

### United By Blue
FASHION & ACCESSORIES

**43** 🔒 MAP P36, D2

At the flagship store of this environmentally conscious fashion brand you can peruse its range of clothing and outdoor goods made from recycled polyester, organic cotton and wool. You can also sip coffee or grab a meal at the appealing cafe. For every product sold, United By Blue promises to remove one pound of trash from the world's oceans and waterways. (☏267-457-3114; https://unitedbyblue.com; 205 Race St, Old City; ⊙7am-7pm Mon-Fri, 8am-7pm Sat & Sun; Ⓢ2nd St)

# Explore ⊙

# Chinatown & Center City East

The star features of this central slice of Philly include a couple of foodie destinations: the historic Reading Terminal Market (p54) and the fourth-largest Chinatown in the USA. LGBT+ visitors will feel at home in the 'Gayborhood,' also known as Midtown Village, a compact area roughly bounded by Walnut, Spruce, Broad and 11th Sts. Washington Sq West is a mostly residential area where you'll find a couple of large hospitals and Jewelry Row.

Get the most out of your visit to Reading Terminal Market by signing up for the twice-weekly Taste of Philly Food Tour. Joining an hour-long tour is the only way to see inside the area's other top attraction, the Masonic Temple (p58). A couple more cultural storehouses – the African American Museum in Philadelphia (p58) and the Fabric Workshop & Museum (p58) – each have their individual appeal. In terms of urban people-watching, Chinatown is also worth a meander.

## Getting There & Around

🚌 Long-distance buses arrive and depart from the Greyhound Terminal. SEPTA buses crisscross these neighborhoods. Access the PHLASH bus along Market St.

**S** Market-Frankford Line subway stations include 15th, 13th and 8th Sts. Broad Street Line trains stop at City Hall, where they connect with the trolley to 13th St.

🚌 Access SEPTA Regional Rail lines at the underground Jefferson Station. The PATCO line for New Jersey has stations at 9th/10th St and 12/13th St.

### Neighborhood map on p56

Chinese Friendship Gate (p61) HELEN89/SHUTTERSTOCK ©

## Top Sight 📷
# Reading Terminal Market

*Keeping the balance right between food market and dining destination, Reading Terminal Market dates back to 1893 and is a city institution. The 75 local stalls crammed into 75,000 sq ft provide a strong flavor of Philly's cultural melting pot, embracing everything from Pennsylvania Dutch to Thai cuisine and attracting everyone from billionaires to blue-collar workers.*

◎ MAP P56, C3

☎ 215-922-2317

www.readingterminal
market.org

51 N 12th St, Center City

◷ 8am-6pm

Ⓢ 11th or 13th St,
🚆 Jefferson

## Market Highlights

The market is open daily but stalls run by Amish and Mennonite families are closed on Sundays. Among the many highlights are:

**Bassetts** America's oldest ice-cream company, established in 1861.

**Miller's Twist** Known for buttery pretzels.

**DiNic's** Tuck into its succulent roast-pork sandwich.

**Hershell's East Side Deli** Jewish soul-food favorites including corned-beef sandwiches and kosher apple cake.

**Pearl's Oyster Bar** Freshly shucked oysters, spicy pepper pot and snapper-turtle soups.

**Beiler's** Hot-from-the-fryer doughnuts and apple fritters, plus breads and barrels of pickles.

**Valley Shepherd Creamery & Meltcraft** Grilled cheese sandwiches made from locally produced cheeses.

**Little Thai Market** Expect a long line for its takeaway dishes such as pad Thai noodles and vegetable red curry ($7).

**PA General Store** (www.pageneralstore. com) Stocking both food and non-food items produced in the state.

## Food Tour

Snack and learn Philly food lore during the 75-minute **Taste of Philly Food Tour** (☎800-838-3006, 215-545-8007; www.tasteofphillyfoodtour. com; adult/child $17/10; ⏰10am Wed & Sat) around Reading Terminal Market with knowledgeable food writer Carolyn Wyman. Reservations are recommended, particularly in busy holiday periods, but you can also just turn up at the meeting point at the market's Welcome Desk, by the entrance on 12th and Filbert.

### ★ Top Tips

○ Alcoholic beverages are sold at the bar **Molly Malloys** and the **Blue Mountain Vineyards & Cellars** – it's okay to take your drink to the general seating area.

○ **Iovine Brothers Produce** and **OK Produce** are among the cheapest places in the city to buy fresh fruit and vegetables.

### ✕ Take a Break

Set yourself up for a tour of the market with a hearty breakfast at the **Dutch Eating Place** (☎ 215-922-0425; mains $4-8; ⏰ 8am-3pm Tue-Wed, to 5pm Thu-Sat).

The roast-pork sandwich at **DiNic's** is the gold standard but don't overlook their slow-roasted beef brisket or Italian-style pulled-pork versions.

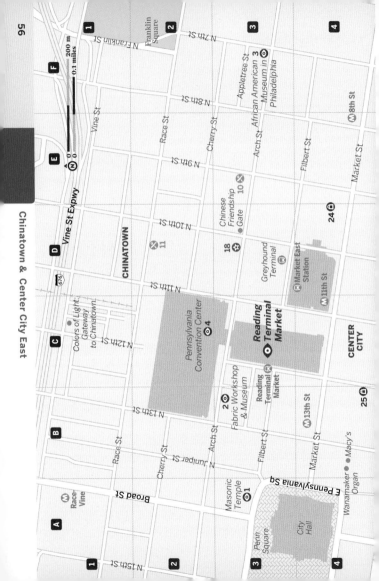

200 m
0.1 miles

Franklin Square

N 7th St

African American 3
Museum in
Philadelphia

Appletree St

M 8th St

N 8th St

Arch St

Filbert St

Market St

Cherry St

Chinese
Friendship
Gate

Race St

N 9th St

⊗ 10

N 10th St

CHINATOWN

⊗ 11

18 ⊗

Greyhound
Terminal

Market East
Station

M 11th St

Vine St

Vine St Expwy

676

Colors of Light:
Gateway
to Chinatown

N 11th St

N 12th St

Pennsylvania
Convention Center

⊙ 4

Reading
Terminal
Market

⊙ Reading
Terminal
Market

CENTER
CITY

24 ⊕

25 ⊕

Fabric Workshop
& Museum

2 ⊙

N 13th St

M 13th St

Filbert St

Market St

Race St

Cherry St

Arch St

N Juniper St

Masonic
Temple

⊙ 1

Broad St

Penn
Square

City
Hall

E Pennsylvania Sq

Wanamaker ● Macy's
Organ

M Race-
Vine

N 15th St

F

E

D

C

B

A

1

2

3

4

Chinatown & Center City East

**For reviews see**

| | | |
|---|---|---|
| ⊙ | Top Sights | p54 |
| ⊙ | Sights | p58 |
| ⊗ | Eating | p59 |
| ⊗ | Drinking | p61 |
| ⊗ | Entertainment | p63 |
| ⊙ | Shopping | p63 |

Washington Square

WASHINGTON SQUARE WEST

Chestnut St

Ranstead Street

Sansom St

Walnut St

Jewelers' Row

8 ⊗

19 ⊙

6 ⊗

Locust St

Spruce St

Pine St

Clinton St

S 7th St
S 8th St
S 9th St
S 10th St
S 11th St

Historic Antique Row

S Quince St

22 ⊙

The Bike Stop

21 ⊙

20 ⊙

Chestnut St

Sansom St

23 ⊙

15 ⊗

17 ⊙

14

Walnut St

Woody's

Chancellor St

Voyeur

U Bar
7 ⊗

Tavern on Camac

9 ⊗

Camac St

12 ⊗

5 ⊗

13 ⊙

16 ⊙

Locust St

Spruce St

Pine St

S 12th St
S 13th St

Toasted
Walnut Bar
& Kitchen

Walnut-Locust St Ⓜ

Broad St

S Juniper St

# Sights

## Masonic Temple
HISTORIC BUILDING

1 ⊙ MAP P56, A3

Although the fortress-like exterior of this 1873 building is pretty impressive, it's the spectacular interiors – which took a further 15 years to complete – that really blow visitors away. Fans of secret societies and theatrical design will be in raptures as each meeting room sports an astonishingly detailed theme – Moorish, Egyptian, Renaissance and more. (☏215-988-1917; https://pamasonictemple.org; 1 N Broad St, Center City; adult/child $15/5; ⊙tours 10am, 11pm, 1pm, 2pm & 3pm Tue-Sat; Ⓢ13th, 15th or City Hall)

## Fabric Workshop & Museum
MUSEUM

2 ⊙ MAP P56, B3

The only such organization of its kind in the US is a wonderful place to discover how creative artists and craftspeople can be with textiles and fabrics. Founded in 1977, it has hosted an artist-in-residence program that has attracted figures of the caliber of Louise Bourgeois, Dale Chihuly and Roy Lichtenstein. Many of the astonishing works can be viewed in the museum as well as bought in the shop. (☏215-561-8888; http://fabricworkshopand museum.org; 1214 Arch St, Center City; suggested donation $5; ⊙10am-6pm Mon-Fri, noon-6pm Sat & Sun; Ⓢ11th or 13th St, Ⓡ Jefferson)

## African American Museum in Philadelphia
MUSEUM

3 ⊙ MAP P56, F3

Founded in 1976, this was the first museum in the country built by a major city to house exhibitions on the life and work of African Americans. Exhibits include ones on notable African American Philadelphians, such as Richard Allen and Octavius Catto, and the Underground Railroad, which assisted slaves in their search for freedom. (☏215-574-0380; www.aampmuseum. org; 701 Arch St, Chinatown; adult/child $14/10; ⊙10am-5pm Wed-Sat, from noon Sun; 🚻; Ⓢ Chinatown or 8th St)

## Pennsylvania Convention Center
CENTER

4 ⊙ MAP P56, C2

Opened in 1993 and expanded in 2011, this massive convention center hosts a busy program of events from the mayor's masked ball and annual horticultural shows to tattoo conventions and travel shows. Enter from Market St and you'll see that it incorporates the old **terminal shed** of the Reading Railroad. This is the only surviving single-span arched train shed in the US and was the largest single-span structure in the world when completed in the 1890s. (☏215-418-4700; www.paconvention.com; 1101 Arch St, Chinatown; Ⓢ11th, 13th or City Hall, Ⓡ Jefferson)

# Eating

## Vetri Cucina ITALIAN $$$

5  MAP P56, A7

Legendary – and for good reason. Since 1998 Marc Vetri has been winning awards and adoring fans with his Italian cuisine. This elegant, intimate restaurant runs like a well-oiled machine and its four-course dinner tasting menu, featuring top-quality seasonal ingredients, rarely disappoints. Don't, on any account, leave without sampling Vetri's famous sweet onion crepe.

Booking well ahead is essential; the three-course lunch on Friday is a great deal for food of this quality and it's often easier to get a reservation then. (☏215-732-3478; https:// vetricucina.com; 1312 Spruce St, Midtown Village; lunch/dinner set menu $85/165; ⏲6-9:30pm Mon-Thu, 11:30am-1pm & 5:45-9:45pm Fri, 5:45-9:45pm Sat, 5-9pm Sun; Ⓢ Walnut-Locust)

## CHeU Noodle Bar ASIAN $$

6  MAP P56, D7

Your Japanese/Korean/Jewish grandmother might not approve, but the brisket ramen with smoked matzo ball and kimchi at CHeU gets our thumbs up. Gleefully mashing up cooking traditions is what this punk-meets-manga kind of place is all about. (☏267-639-4136; www.cheunoodlebar.com; 255 S 10th St, Washington Sq West; ⏲11:30am-2:30pm & 5-10pm Mon-Thu, to 11pm Fri, noon-11pm Sat, to 10pm Sun; 🚌12, 47m)

Dirty Franks (p61) mural by David McShane, Mural Arts Philadelphia

Chinatown & Center City East Eating

## Vedge

VEGAN $$

7 ✕ MAP P56, B6

Since 2011 Vedge has been setting the standard not only for vegan restaurants in Philly but restaurants in general. A meal here will crush any misconceptions you may have about the lack of flavor or finesse in vegan dishes. Flavors are punchy, presentation and inventiveness first-rate. Items not to miss include its rutabaga fondue and sumptuous sorbets. (☑215-320-7500; http://vedgerestaurant.com; 1221 Locust St, Midtown Village; mains $14-16; ⊘5-10pm Mon-Thu, to 11pm Fri & Sat; ⊀; Ⓢ Walnut-Locust)

## Morimoto

JAPANESE $$$

8 ✕ MAP P56, E5

Morimoto is high-concept and heavily stylized, from a dining room that looks like a futuristic aquarium to a menu of globe-spanning influences and eclectic combinations. A meal at this *Iron Chef* regular's restaurant is a theatrical experience. (☑215-413-9070; www.morimotorestaurant.com; 723 Chestnut St, Washington Sq West; mains $29-46; ⊘11:30am-2pm & 5-10pm Mon-Thu, to midnight Fri & Sat, 5-10pm Sun; ⊀; Ⓢ 8th St)

## Mercato

ITALIAN $$

9 ✕ MAP P56, B7

It's cash-only and BYOB at this popular place that's very cozy and usually packed to the gills with a chatty crowd – making it no place for an intimate, romantic meal. The rustic Italian food is largely traditional, seasonal and served in good-sized portions. (☑215-985-2962; www.mercatobyob.com; 1216 Spruce St, Midtown Village; 🚌12, 23)

## Rangoon

BURMESE $

10 ✕ MAP P56, E3

Sample Burmese specialties, such as Shan noodle soup and Asian tea leaf salad, at this reliable Chinatown restaurant. Among the huge array of tantalizing specialties are spicy red-bean shrimp, curried chicken with egg noodles, and coconut tofu. (☑215-829-8939; www.rangoonrestaurant.com; 112 N 9th St, Chinatown; mains $7-18.50; ⊘11:30am-9pm Sun-Thu, to 10pm Fri & Sat; Ⓢ Chinatown or 8th St)

## Nan Zhou Hand Drawn Noodle House

CHINESE $

11 ✕ MAP P56, D2

It's cash only and BYOB at this hand-pulled noodle joint. Slurp up

### Famous Franks Mural

The walls outside Dirty Franks are decorated with this witty mural by David McShane featuring Frank Sinatra, Frank Zappa, Aretha Franklin, Benjamin Franklin, architects Frank Furness and Frank Lloyd Wright among several other 'Franks'. In 2015, McShane added Pope Francis following his visit to the city that year.

## Philadelphia's Chinatown

When the Pennsylvania Convention Center was constructed in the early 1990s, much of the adjacent Chinatown was demolished. However, this distinct enclave, which has existed since the 1860s, endures. Its flavor is now more pan-Asian as reflected in the Asian, Burmese, Thai, Vietnamese and Japanese businesses and restaurants you'll encounter here.

At the junction with Arch St and marking the entrance to Chinatown, the 40ft **Chinese Friendship Gate** (Map p56, D3; N 10th St; S 11th St) was built in 1984 in part by artisans from Philadelphia's sister city of Tianjin. It's decorated with dragon and flower motifs, small animal sculptures and ornamental roof tiles.

Also look out for the mural **Colors of Light: Gateway to Chinatown** (Map p56, C1; www.muralarts.org/artworks/gateway-to-chinatown-colors-of-light; 23, S Chinatown). Bursting out the side of a building on the corner of Vine and 12th Sts, this 1999 Mural Arts project features a flying dragon, playing kids and Chinese scroll.

delicious and inexpensive soups with perfectly chewy noodles, plus standard stir-fries. (215-923-1550; www.nanzhounoodlehouse.com; 1022 Race St, Chinatown; mains $6-10; 11am-10pm daily; S Race-Vine or Chinatown)

### Bud & Marilyn's
SOUTHERN US $$

12 MAP P56, B6

Darkly lit with a mid-century modern style, this place channels 1950s Americana. Southern-style cooking offers up succulent deep-fried chicken with warm biscuits and zucchini pickles, as well as hot buttered rolls. There's counter and booth seating, and good happy-hour specials from 5pm to 7pm weekdays, with some that kick in again after 10pm. (215-546-2220; http://budandmarilyns.com; 1234 Locust St, Midtown Village; mains $24; noon-3pm & 5-11pm Mon-Thu, to midnight Fri, 10am-3pm & 5pm-midnight Sat, 10am-3pm & 5-11pm Sun; S Walnut-Locust)

## Drinking

### Dirty Franks
BAR

13 MAP P56, A8

In business since 1933, Franks' regulars call this bar an 'institution' with some irony, but it does have grunge style as well as housing the Off The Wall gallery. Like many Philly dives, it offers the 'citywide special': a shot of Jim Beam and a can of PBR for $2.50. Need cheaper? Try the 'DF Shelf of Shame' beer for just two bucks! (215-732-5010; www.dirtyfranksbar.com; 347 S 13th St, Washington Sq West; 11am-2am; 23, 40)

### Wanamaker Organ

📷

**Macy's** (Map p56, B4; 📞215-241-9000; https://l.macys.com/philadelphia-pa; 1300 Market St, Center City; ⊙10am-8pm Mon-Thu, 9am-10pm Fri & Sat, 11am-8pm Sun; 🚇; ⑤11th St, 🚆Jefferson) is the latest tenant for what was once Wanamaker's, one of the US's first department stores. The sales floors fan out around a spectacular five-story tall Grand Court, in the middle of which you'll find *Eagle*, a giant 1904 bronze by August Gaul. Come here also to hear the free concerts given on the **Wanamaker Organ** (📞484-684 7250; www.wanamakerorgan.com; ⊙concerts noon Mon-Sat, also 5:30pm Mon, Tue, Thu & Sat, 7pm Wed & Fri), the second largest operational pipe organ in the world.

### Double Knot

BAR

14 🚇 MAP P56, B5

This is one of the few places in Philly that serves sake properly (poured into an overflowing cup inside a wooden *masu* container). They also makes great craft cocktails and have a delicious food menu. It can get crowded, but the stylish decor and friendly service make it a fun spot to grab a bite and late-night drink.

From 5pm they open up the basement, which hides an impressive Japanese restaurant with a sushi bar and *robatayaki* (flame-grilled cooked items). (📞215-631-3868; www.doubleknotphilly.com; 120 S 13th St, Midtown Village; ⊙7am-midnight; ⑤13th St or Walnut-Locust)

### Charlie Was a Sinner   COCKTAIL BAR

15 🚇 MAP P56, B5

Charlie, apparently, sinned during the building's sketchy past as a brothel. Never mind, it's a catchy name for what is now a sophisticated cocktail bar and restaurant where food and booze are both vegan. Watch the mixologist blowtorch wood chips to create the smoke that perfumes some of the bar's creations. (📞267-758-5372; http://charliewasasinner.com; 131 S 13th St, Midtown Village; ⊙4pm-2am; ⑤Walnut-Locust or 13th St)

### Writer's Block Rehab   COCKTAIL BAR

16 🚇 MAP P56, A7

Cafe by day, cocktail bar by night, this quirky bar, just south of the Gayborhood, is a bit of a gem. Wordsmiths will love its trompe l'oeil library wallpaper, chandeliers made of vintage globes and menus in hardcover books – all showing a dedication to the literary theme. It's a cool spot for a quiet drink whether you're blocked or not. (📞267-603-6960; www.facebook.com/writersblockrehab/; 1342 Cypress St, Midtown Village; ⊙8am-noon & 4-10pm Mon-Thu, 8am-noon & 3pm-

1am Fri, noon-1am Sat, noon-11pm Sun; **S** Walnut-Locust)

## McGillin's Olde Ale House
IRISH PUB

**17 🕒 MAP P56, A5**

Philadelphia's oldest continually operating tavern (since 1860) – it remained open as a speakeasy in the Prohibition years – is a chummy Irish-style pub with karaoke on Wednesdays and Sundays and an open mic on Thursdays. Find it tucked away down an alley. ( 📞 215-735-5562; www.mcgillins.com; 1310 Drury St, Midtown Village; 🕐 11am-2am; **S** 13th St or Walnut-Locust)

# Entertainment

## Trocadero Theater
LIVE MUSIC

**18 ⭐ MAP P56, D3**

Affectionately known as the Troc, this old movie theater is mainly used for rock and pop concerts and comedy shows these days. However, it reverts to its original use every Monday with a great deal on classic, geek and cult cinema screenings, where the $3 ticket cost goes toward your choice of drink or snack. ( 📞 215-922-6888; www.thetroc.com; 1003 Arch St, Chinatown; **S** 11th St, 🚇 Jefferson)

## Walnut Street Theater
THEATER

**19 ⭐ MAP P56, E6**

Dating back to 1809, this is the nation's oldest playhouse and was designated a National Historic Landmark in 1964. Many stars of yesteryear trod the boards here including Helen Hayes, Edward G Robinson, Jack Lemmon and Katharine Hepburn. The venue includes the Mainstage and smaller Independence Studio on 3. ( 📞 215-574-3550; www.walnutstreettheatre.org; 825 Walnut St, Washington Square West; **S** 8th St)

# Shopping

## Ten Thousand Villages
ARTS & CRAFTS

**20 🔒 MAP P56, C6**

Browse a globe-trotting selection of goods at this ethically-focused handicrafts store supporting fair-trade initiatives around the world. Pick up anything from Peruvian woolly hats to singing bowls from Nepal. ( 📞 215-574-2008; www.tenthousandvillages.com; 1122 Walnut St, Midtown Village; 🕐 10am-7pm Mon-Sat, noon-5pm Sun; **S** 11th St, 🚇 Jefferson)

---

### Shopping on Jewelers' Row

It's incredible to think that over 300 retailers, wholesalers and craftspeople in gems and jewelry are crammed into this couple of blocks around the intersection of 8th and **Sansom Sts** (Map p56, E6; www.jrow.org; Washington Sq West; **S** 8th St). This is the oldest and second-largest district in the US specializing in bling, and is where you want to go if jewelery is on your shopping list.

# The Gayborhood

Plastered with rainbow flags, the Gayborhood (aka Midtown Village) is welcoming to all, regardless of gender or sexual orientation – but do bring proper ID (that means a passport for overseas visitors) as most places will check you're old enough to imbibe. Choice spots include:

**Woody's** (Map p56, B6; 215-545-1893; http://woodysbar.com; 202 S 13th St; 7pm-2am; 13th St or Walnut-Locust) Philly's oldest gay bar is fail-safe for good night out. The original bar is supplemented by neighboring connected spaces. On the corner with Walnut St is the spacey **Globar**, while a 'secret passage' provides a connection with the art-deco **Rosewood** cocktail lounge, also opening onto Walnut. Upstairs is the dance bar **Suite**.

**Tavern on Camac** (TOC; Map p56, B7; 215-545-0900; www.tavernon camac.com; 243 S Camac St; piano bar 4pm-2am, restaurant 6pm-1am Wed-Mon, club 9pm-2am Tue-Sun; Walnut-Locust) This long-established joint has a piano bar and restaurant downstairs. Upstairs is **Ascend**, a small club with a dance floor; Wednesday is ladies' night, Friday and Saturday have DJs. And don't overlook Showtune Sunday.

**Toasted Walnut Bar & Kitchen** (Map p56, A6; 215-546-8888; www.facebook.com/toastedwalnutphiladelphia; 1316 Walnut St; 4pm-2am Tue-Sat, from 3pm Sun.; 13th St or Walnut-Locust) Although they don't turn boys away, it's pretty clear this sports bar is one for the girls. Spread over three levels, there's DJs and karaoke depending on the night – check its Facebook page for details.

**U Bar** (Map p56, B6; 215-546-6660; www.ubarphilly.com; 1220 Locust St; 11am-2am; Walnut-Locust) The floor-to-ceiling windows (which open up on warm nights) provide clear views of the comings and goings of the Gayborhood.

**The Bike Stop** (Map p56, C6; 215-627-1662; www.thebikestop. com; 206 S Quince St; 4pm-2am Mon-Sat, 2pm-2am Sun; 13th St or Walnut-Locust) Welcome to Philly's out and proud leather bar with a pool table upstairs, porn on the TVs above the bar and a dungeon in the basement.

**Voyeur** (Map p56, B6; 215-735-5772; www.voyeurnightclub.com; 1221 St James St; cover charge $10-20; midnight-3:30am Tue-Sun; Walnut-Locust) As every other bar around the Gayborhood shuts down at 2am, this dance club starts cranking up. Top DJs spin to a back-ground of chandeliers, lasers and an illuminated runway dance floor.

## Lapstone & Hammer

FASHION & ACCESSORIES

**21** 🔒 MAP P56, C5

Occupying the former home of Pauline's, an old art-deco bridal store, Lapstone & Hammer's range of male streetwear and high fashion is artfully displayed. Among the international labels, such as Comme des Garçon and Adidas, are local brands including Divine Lorraine (named after a storied city hotel) and L&H's own sweatshirts, t-shirts and utility pants. (📞215-592-9166; www.lapstoneandhammer.com; 1106 Chestnut St, Midtown Village; ⏰10am-7pm Mon-Sat, noon-5pm Sun; Ⓢ11th St, 🚇Jefferson)

## Philly AIDS Thrift @ Giovanni's Room

BOOKS

**22** 🔒 MAP P56, B8

Every shape and shade of LGBTQI book and magazine appears to be on sale at this long-running secondhand bookstore. It carries many other book genres, too, as well as some recorded music, clothing and other bits and bobs. Check its website for details of author readings and other events (usually held on weekend evenings). (📞215-923-2960; www.queerbooks.com; 345 S 12th St, Washington Sq West; ⏰11am-8pm Mon-Thu, to 9pm Fri & Sat, to 7pm Sun; 🚌23, 40)

## Duross & Langel

HEALTH & WELLNESS

**23** 🔒 MAP P56, B5

The local equivalent of Body Shop, Duross & Langel produce handcrafted bath and body-care products in a variety of appealing scents and applications at its on-site workshop. Let your nose lead you to the ideal soap, scrub, shower gel or moisturizer. (📞215-834-7226; www.durossandlangel.com; 117 S 13th St, Midtown Village; ⏰11am-7pm Tue, to 8pm Wed & Thu, 10am-7pm Fri & Sat, noon-5pm Sun; Ⓢ13th St or Walnut-Locust)

## Fashion District

MALL

**24** 🔒 MAP P56, D4

Sure to be a game changer on the city's retail scene is this mammoth fashion-focused mall, spanning three blocks along Market St between 8th and 11th Sts. Century 21 and Burlington's outlets are open, with other stores set to open late 2018. (📞215-925-7162; www.fashiondistrictphiladelphia.com; 1101 Market St, Center City East; Ⓢ11th St, 8th St)

## Mitchell & Ness

SPORTS & OUTDOORS

**25** 🔒 MAP P56, B4

The sporting apparel and goods shop that Frank Mitchell and Charles Ness set up in Philly in 1904 has grown to be a national business. This is the chain's flagship store, where you can pick up all the gear for the local teams plus many others, including caps and jerseys. (📞267-273-7622; www.mitchellandness.com; 1201 Chestnut St, entrance on 12th St, Center City; ⏰10am-7pm Mon-Sat, 11am-5pm Sun; Ⓢ11th St or 13th St)

# Explore ◈

# Rittenhouse Square & Center City West

*The area around City Hall is the engine of Philadelphia: all office buildings and big hotels, concert halls and restaurants. A few blocks to the southwest, genteel Rittenhouse Sq is a quiet counterpoint, the center of an elegant residential district dotted with cafes and small restaurants. Between the two are the prime retail strips of Chestnut and Walnut Sts, while the area's western edge is fringed by the cycling and jogging trails of Schuylkill Banks.*

*The area's key sights – City Hall (p72), Pennsylvania Academy of the Fine Arts (p72), Mütter Museum (p72) and Rosenbach Museum & Library (p72) – can all be seen comfortably in a day with some advance planning to check on opening times and tours. Otherwise it's a pleasant area to explore on foot with some great examples of public art.*

## Getting There & Around

🚌 SEPTA buses crisscross these neighborhoods. Access the PHLASH bus around City Hall.

Ⓢ Market-Frankford Line subway stations include 15th & 13th. Broad Street Line trains stop at City Hall (where they connect with the trolley that stops at 13th, 19th and 22nd Sts), Walnut-Locust and Lombard-South.

🚈 At the underground Suburban station access SEPTA Regional Rail lines. The PATCO line for New Jersey has stations at 15th/16th Sts and 12/13th Sts.

### Neighborhood Map on p70

Rittenhouse Square (p74) JON LOVETTE/GETTY IMAGES ©

# Walking Tour 🚶

# Center City Public Art

*Ever since the city commissioned a 37ft bronze statue of William Penn in 1892, public art has been central to Philadelphia's civic project. This walk around Center City takes you past key commissions; build in extra time if you sign up for a tour of City Hall.*

## Walk Facts

**Start** Pennsylvania Academy of the Fine Arts; **S** Race-Vine, City Hall or 15th

**End** Octavius V Catto Memorial; **S** 13th St

**Length** 1 mile, one hour

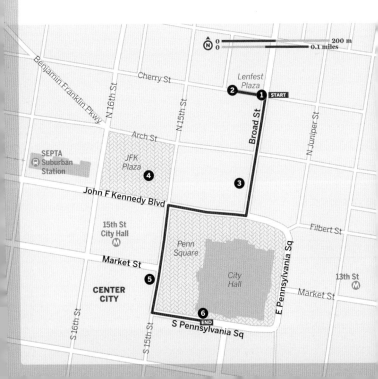

# ❶ Paint Torch

In Lenfest Plaza is this **work** (www.
pafa.org/lenfest-plaza/oldenburgs
-paint-torch; Broad & Cherry Sts;
[S]Race-Vine or City Hall or 15th St) by
Claes Oldenburg, a 51ft fiberglass
paint brush with an accompanying
giant blob of paint.

# ❷ Grumman Greenhouse

Also in Lenfest Plaza, **Grumman
Greenhouse** (www.pafa.org/lenfest
-plaza/grumman-greenhouse; Lenfest
Plaza; [S]Race-Vine or City Hall or 15th
St), by Jordan Griska, is formed
from a Grumman Tracker II
naval plane that appears to have
crash-landed into the ground.
The cockpit and the plane's intact
interior have been turned into a
greenhouse where plants grow.

# ❸ Municipal Services Building Plaza

The broad **plaza** (Broad St; [S]City
Hall or 15th St) opposite City Hall
hosts several public art works
including *Your Move*, by Daniel
Martinez, Renee Petropoulis and
Roger White, which consists of
giant board-game pieces, and the
massive bronze *Government of
the People*, by Jacques Lipchitz,
which represents the struggle for
democracy.

# ❹ JFK Plaza

Have your camera ready for
probably Philly's most popular
selfie location – in front of Robert
Indiana's iconic *LOVE* sculpture
in **JFK Plaza** (Love Park; 16th St
& JFK Blvd; [S]City Hall or 15th St,
[R]Suburban).

# ❺ Clothespin

There's another great shot to be
had beside the giant **Clothespin**
(www.associationforpublicart.org/art
work/clothespin; Center Sq Plaza, cnr
15th & Market Sts; [S]City Hall or 15th
St), a work by Claes Oldenburg.

# ❻ A Quest for Parity: The Octavius V Catto Memorial

This is the first monument in the
city dedicated to an individual
**African American** (www.ovcatto
memorial.org; S Broad St; [S]City Hall
or 15th St). A successful activist
who led the battle to desegregate
Philly's public trolleys, Catto was
just 32 when he was killed on
election day in 1871 while rallying
African American men to vote.

## ✕ Elixir Coffee Roasters

This hopping coffee **spot** (Map
p70, G4; [☎]239-404-1730; www.
elixrcoffee.com; 207 S Sydenham
St, Rittenhouse; ⊙7am-8pm
Mon-Fri, 8am-7pm Sat & Sun; [?];
[S]Walnut-Locust) has a warehouse theme, complete with
meat-locker doors for the bath-
rooms. Good wi-fi and quality
hand-dripped coffees make it a
fun stop for that cup of joe.

**76** A

30th St
Schuylkill River

John F Kennedy Blvd

1
Schuylkill Expwy

22nd St

Market St

N 23rd St
N 22nd St
N 21st St
N 20th St

S 24th St
S 23rd St
S 22nd St

**4**
Mütter Museum

2

Chestnut St

21st St
S 20th St

Ludlow St

**17**

Sansom St

S 16th St

5
Schuylkill Banks

**8**

3

Walnut St

**21**

Church of the Holy Trinity
Rittenhouse Square

Locust St

Rittenhouse Sq **7**

Rittenhouse Sq ● Cook

Manning St

4

Spruce St

**13**

S 24th St
S 23rd St
S 22nd St
S 21st St
S 20th St
S 19th St

Delancey Pl

**3**
Rosenbach Museum & Library

5

Lombard St

South St

6

Bainbridge St

**For reviews see**
| | | |
|---|---|---|
| ◉ Sights | p72 |
| ⊗ Eating | p74 |
| ⊖ Drinking | p76 |
| ✪ Entertainment | p79 |
| ⊖ Shopping | p80 |

A    B    C    D

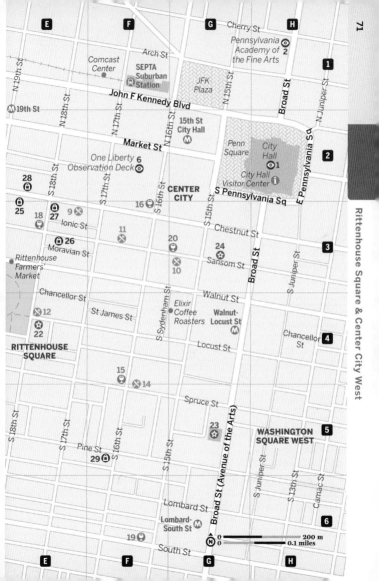

# Sights

## City Hall

NOTABLE BUILDING

**1** MAP P70, H2

Completed in 1901 following 30 years of construction, City Hall takes up a whole block, and at 548ft is the world's tallest structure without a steel frame. The view from the observation area immediately beneath the 27-ton bronze statue of William Penn that crowns the tower takes in most of the city (reserve tickets ahead as space is limited). The daily interior tour is a treat, too, and will give you a greater appreciation of this grand building.

In winter, there's **ice-skating** (www.rothmaninstitute.com; adult/child $5/3, skate rental $10; ⏰noon-9pm Mon-Thu, to 11pm Fri, 11am-11pm Sat, 11am-8pm Sun mid-Nov–late Feb) in Dilworth Park on the west side of the plaza. (☏215-686-2840; www.phlvisitorcenter.com; cnr Broad & Market Sts; tower adult/student $8/4, interior & tower adult/student $15/8; ⏰tower tours every 15min 9:30am-4:15pm, interior tour 12:30pm Mon-Fri; Ⓢ City Hall & 15th St)

## Pennsylvania Academy of the Fine Arts

MUSEUM

**2** MAP P70, H1

This prestigious arts school, founded in 1805, occupies two buildings including a masterwork of Victorian Gothic architecture designed by Frank Furness and George Hewitt. Start your tour of the museum's collection in that building, where the interior design warily tied – but not quite – overshadows the works on display. The key piece is *The Gross Clinic* by Thomas Eakins, a former student and later teacher at the academy. (☏215-972-7600; www.pafa.org; 118-128 N Broad St, Center City; adult/student/child $15/8/free; ⏰10am-5pm Tue-Fri, 11am-5pm Sat & Sun; Ⓢ Race-Vine, City Hall & 15th)

## Rosenbach Museum & Library

MUSEUM

**3** MAP P70, C5

The list of famous authors in the collection here could fill a book itself: Edgar Allan Poe, James Joyce, Maurice Sendak, George Washington, Lewis Carroll, Bram Stoker...to name a few. If you fancy a peek at *Ulysses,* this is the place. Admission includes a guided tour through the museum and library.

Hands-on tours, which allow access to rare and important items not usually on view to the public, are offered at 3pm most Fridays and Sundays (registration two weeks in advance is necessary). (☏215-732-1600; https://rosenbach.org; 2008-2010 Delancy Pl, Rittenhouse; adult/child $10/5; ⏰noon-5pm Tue & Fri, to 8pm Wed & Thu, to 6pm Sat & Sun; 🚌17)

## Mütter Museum

MUSEUM

**4** MAP P70, C2

Maintained by the College of Physicians, this unique, only-in-Philadelphia attraction is a museum dedicated to rare, odd or disturbing medical conditions. Not for the squeamish, its nonetheless fascinating exhibits include a saponified body, a conjoined female fetus, incredibly realistic wax models of medical conditions, and skulls by the dozen. (☎215-560-8564; www.muttermuseum.org; 19 S 22nd St, Rittenhouse; adult/child $18/13; ☺10am-5pm; 🚇22nd St)

## Schuylkill Banks

PARK

5 ◉ MAP P70, A3

This wonderful outdoor recreation area covers around 8 miles of Schuylkill River, mostly on the east bank from below the Fairmount Dam through the heart of Philadelphia. Dedicated cycling and jogging trails have been created, and various other activities hap-

pen throughout the year, including outdoor movie screenings, yoga, and kayak and boat tours – check the website for details. (www.schuylkillbanks.org; entrances off Walnut St & 25th St, Schuylkill River; 🚍9, 12, 21, 42, 🚇22nd St)

## One Liberty Observation Deck

OBSERVATORY

6 ◉ MAP P70, F2

One way to get a bird's-eye view of the city, especially pretty after dark, is to ride the ear-popping elevator up to this 883ft-high observation deck on the 57th floor of One Liberty Place. There are tickets allowing two visits within 48 hours and family deals, as well as online discounts. (Philly From the Top; ☎215-561-3325;

One Liberty Observation Deck

GONZALO AZUMENDI/GETTY IMAGES ©

Rittenhouse Square & Center City West Sights

## Mural Arts Tours

In 1984 artist Jane Golden was hired by the Anti-Graffiti Network to co-opt graffiti writers in helping create public murals across the city. In the three decades since the Mural Art Program was established, it has gifted over 3000 murals to Philadelphia, tackling important social issues and creating an outdoor art gallery that is unparalleled in the world.

The program aims to empower communities, who get to choose the theme of their murals, and helps spark economic revitalization. Life skills and pride are also provided to some of society's most marginalized folk, including disadvantaged kids and prisoners, by having them participate in the creation of the artworks.

To fully appreciate the transformative nature of the Mural Arts Program to the city and its people, join one of its **tours** (☑215-925-3633; www.muralarts.org/tours; tours $23-32), most of which start from the lobby of the Pennsylvania Academy of the Fine Arts (p72). Between April and Thanksgiving, these walking or trolley-based tours are led by enthusiastic and knowledgeable guides, and cover murals in a specific location or on a particular theme.

The Mural Mile, a free self-guided tour and map, is available online.

http://phillyfromthetop.com; 1650 Market St, Center City; adult/child $14.50/9.50; ☺10am-8pm)

### Rittenhouse Sq

SQUARE

7 ◉ MAP P70, D4

One of five original squares planned by city founder William Penn in the late 17th century, and the most prestigious, this square was named after David Rittenhouse, the 18th-century astronomer, mathematician and clockmaker. It features a fine collection of bronze statues, a kids' wading pool and benches beneath shady trees. (http://friendsofrittenhouse.org; 1800 Walnut St, Rittenhouse; 🚌9, 12, 17, 21, 42, 🚇19th St)

# Eating

### V Street

VEGAN $$

8 ✕ MAP P70, D3

Street food from around the world is the influence for the fab vegan menu here. Make sure you sample the delicious dan dan noodles, in which the spices are not dialed down; you will break out in a sweat in a good way. There are plenty of counter seats for single diners. (☑215-278-7943; http://vstreetfood.com; 126 S 19th St, Rittenhouse; mains $13-14; ☺5-10pm Mon-Thu, 11am-3pm & 5-10pm Fri-Sun; 🖉; 🚌9, 17 21, 42, 🚇19th St)

## Gran Caffè L'Aquila

ITALIAN $$$

9 MAP P70, E3

Mamma mia, this is impressive Italian food. Not only are the flavors everything you could ask for, one of the owners is an award-winning gelato maker and the 2nd floor has its own gelato factory. Some of the main courses even have savory gelato as a garnish. Coffee is house-roasted and the dapper waitstaff are eager to please. (215-568-5600; http://grancaffelaquila.com; 1716 Chestnut St, Rittenhouse; mains $18-30; 7am-10pm Mon-Thu, to 11pm Fri, 8am-11pm Sat, to 10pm Sun, bar open 1hr later; 9, 21, 42, 19th St)

## Rooster Soup Co

AMERICAN $

10 MAP P70, G3

Its chicken soup with smoked matzo balls is legendary, and it's great that you can rock up anytime for the all-day brunch items. But the best part of this basement-level classic-styled diner is that 100% of its profits support vulnerable locals through the volunteer kitchen charity Broad Street Ministry. (215-454-6939; www.roostersoupcompany.com; 1526 Sansom St, Center City; mains $6-13; 11am-8pm Mon-Fri, 10am-8pm Sat & Sun; City Hall & 15th St, Suburban)

## Abe Fisher

JEWISH $$

11 MAP P70, F3

Chef Yehuda Sichel's menu riffs on the foods of the Jewish diaspora, offering quirky, punchy takes on staples such as cholent (a beef stew) served as a potpie, and veal schnitzel in tacos. It's all small plates, shareable and with free-flowing sparkling water. (215-867-0088; http://abefisherphilly.com; 1623 Sansom St, Rittenhouse; small

## Comcast Center

This glass-clad 58-story **tower** (Map p70, F1; 215-496-1810; www.themarketandshopsatcomcastcenter.com; 1701 John F Kennedy Blvd, Center City; admission free; 8am-7pm Mon-Fri, to 5pm Sat; City Hall & 15th St, Suburban) is one of the tallest 'green' buildings in the US. Its 140ft-tall atrium lobby is the location of Humanity in Motion, a beguiling work consisting of 10 horizontal poles criss-crossing the space on which life-sized figures balance like tightrope walkers.

Chance are that your attention will first be grabbed by the mesmerizing series of high-res video images playing out on the 2000-sq-ft LED screen that is also here. The 18-hour-long video never repeats itself and is never the same twice. Below ground level is a food court and shopping mall, which links directly to Suburban railway station.

## Cook 🍴

Book well ahead for the classes at **Cook** (Map p70, D4; ☎215-735-2665; http://audreyclairecook.com; 253 S 20 St, Rittenhouse; lunch/dinner classes from $85/160; 🚇12, 17), featuring leading up-and-coming and under-the-radar local chefs. In a beautifully designed teaching studio/dining room, these are mainly demonstrations – so more watching and taking notes than hands on. Dinners include all wines and tips. The daytime classes are mainly held on weekends.

plates $13-18, 3-course prix-fixe $39; ⏱5-10pm Mon-Thu, to 11pm Fri & Sat, to 9pm Sun; Ⓢ City Hall & 15th St, 🚇Suburban)

### Parc Brasserie          FRENCH $$$

12 🍴 MAP P70, E4

Soak up the elegant Rittenhouse Sq vibe at this enormous, polished bistro right on the park. Dinner is a little steep, but brunch and lunch are good value, and prime people-watching time. For dessert, try the beer float (lambic, to get technical). Yum! (☎215-545-2262; www.parc-restaurant.com; 227 S 18th St, Rittenhouse; mains from $23; ⏱7:30am-11pm, to midnight Fri, 10am-midnight Sat, to 10pm Sun; 🚇9, 12, 17, 21, 42)

## Metropolitan Cafe & Bakery          CAFE $

13 🍴 MAP P70, D4

Great breads, tender pastries and good coffee make for a perfect breakfast or lunch at this flagship location of Metropolitan. It's also famous for its granola. The cafe here is closed on Monday. (☎215-545-6655; www.metropolitanbakery.com; 262 S 19th St, Rittenhouse; sandwiches from $9.50, pizza $15-17; ⏱7:30am-7pm Mon-Fri, 8am-6pm Sat & Sun; 🚇9, 12, 17, 21, 42)

### Russet          MEDITERRANEAN $$

14 🍴 MAP P70, F5

Russet stands out from the other charming BYOB restaurants across the neighborhood for its expert renditions of French and Italian dishes using fresh seasonal ingredients. There are always a trio of handmade pasta dishes on the menu, which changes daily. (☎215-546-1521; www.russetphilly.com; 1521 Spruce St, Rittenhouse; mains $24-30; ⏱5:30-9:30pm Tue-Thu, to 10:30pm Fri, 11am-2pm & 5:30-9pm Sat & Sun; 🚇2, 12)

# Drinking

## Monk's Cafe          BAR

15 🍴 MAP P70, F4

Hop fans crowd this mellow wood-paneled place for Belgian and American craft beers on tap – it has one of the best selections in the city. For those needing assistance, a 'Beer Bible' is available.

There's also a reasonably priced food menu, with typical mussels-and-fries as well as a daily vegan special. (☏215-545-7005; www. monkscafe.com; 264 S 16th St, Rittenhouse; ⊙11:30am-2am, kitchen to 1am; ⓢWalnut-Locust)

## R2L Restaurant LOUNGE

16 🔘 MAP P70, F3

The view, the view, the view. And did we mention the view? This upscale spot serves up the night-scape of Philly along with whatever is on the menu. Craft cocktails are smooth and balanced, but even tap water would seem ritzy when you're looking out at the cosmos of lights below you. (☏215-564-5337; https://r2lrestaurant.com; 50 S 16th St, Center City; ⊙lounge 4pm-1am Mon-Thu, 4pm-2am Fri & Sat, 4-11pm Sun; ⓢCity Hall & 15th St, ᕮSuburban)

## Ranstead Room LOUNGE

17 🔘 MAP P70, D2

This popular speakeasy stays on the down low with no website and no clear sign – look for the double R on the door. Inside it's all dim lights, red and black wallpaper, and great craft cocktails, making it a good choice for those seeking somewhere cozy and intimate. The menu is great, but bartender's choice is better. (☏215-563-3330; 2013 Ranstead St, Rittenhouse; ⊙6pm-2am; 🚌9, 17, 21, 42, 🚆19th St)

Parc Brasserie

## Race Matters

Research has shown that Philadelphia is one of the most segregated cities in the US, as well as one of the poorest. The geographical and economic divisions between different ethnic groups in Philly are stark and controversial.

In 2013 when *Philadelphia* magazine ran a feature by Robert Huber entitled 'Being White in Philly' it sparked a heated public debate, and not a little soul searching, over the state of race relations in the city of brotherly love. Then mayor Michael Nutter slammed the feature claiming it was irresponsible and inflammatory, while the magazine's editor hit back citing free speech and a need to encourage a deeper discussion about race.

More recently, the Black Lives Matter movement has upped the ante on such discussions. One of its targets has been the statue of controversial former mayor Frank Rizzo. Activist Asa Khalif voiced the feelings of the wider black community when he claimed that the statue was representative of decades of oppression and violence. In November 2017 the city announced the statue would be removed from its prominent location facing City Hall.

### Dandelion
PUB

18 MAP P70, E3

The bustling atmosphere of an English country inn and great food set this gastropub apart, and the bar is open until 2am. Craft cocktails, such as the Pimm's Deluxe, are fun, and the plethora of beer options (draft and bottled) mean there's something for everyone. (215-558-2500; http://thedandelionpub.com; 124 S 18th St, Rittenhouse; beers $4; 11:30am-2am Mon-Fri, 10am-2am Sat & Sun; 9, 12, 17, 21, 42, 19th St)

### Bob & Barbara's Lounge
LOUNGE

19 MAP P70, F6

This classic dive with a padded linoleum bar and lots of Pabst Blue Ribbon–themed decor is named after its original owner and manager. They're long gone but the Philly 'special' (PBR and a shot of Jim Beam for just $3) is a permanent fixture. Don't come expecting fancy, but plan on having a good time. (215-545-4511; www.bobandbarbaras.com; 1509 South St, Graduate Hospital; 3pm-2am; Lombard-South)

## Harp & Crown BAR

20 🚇 MAP P70, G3

It's tempting to hang out upstairs at this buzzing restaurant and bar with its double-height ceiling and long horseshoe bar. But head downstairs to discover the two-lane bowling alley and cozy gentleman's club–like space with leather armchairs and distressed walls. There's a good range of cocktails from $11 and draft beer from $7. (☎215-330-2800; http://harpcrown.com; 1525 Sansom St, Rittenhouse; ⏱5pm-midnight, last food order 10pm; S City Hall, 15th St or Walnut-Locust)

## Tria Taproom CRAFT BEER

21 🚇 MAP P70, D3

Focused on draft beers (around 20 of them), with geeky but elegant style, Tria Taproom offers good food carefully designed to match what's on tap. It also has cider, craft soda, a few wines and even kombucha. (☎215-557-8277; www.triaphilly.com; 2005 Walnut St, Rittenhouse; ⏱noon-1am; 🚌9, 12, 21, 42, 🚊19th St)

# Entertainment

## Curtis Institute of Music CLASSICAL MUSIC

22 ⭐ MAP P70, E4

One of the finest music conservatories in the world, the Curtis only accepts exceptionally gifted students into its tuition-free programs. If you attend one of the free student recitals (highly recommended!), mainly of solo and chamber works, you'll witness some extraordinary performances in the institute's elegant wood-paneled Field Concert Hall. (☎215-893-7902; www.curtis.edu; 1726 Locust St, Rittenhouse; student recitals admission free; ⏱8pm most Mon, Wed & Fri; 🚌9, 12, 17, 21, 42, S Walnut-Locust)

## Kimmel Center PERFORMING ARTS

23 ⭐ MAP P70, G5

The city's most prestigious arts institution, this modern concert hall, designed by Rafael Viñoly, hosts the Philadelphia Orchestra, the Pennsylvania Ballet and more. A giant barrel-shaped glass roof encloses two main auditoriums: the 2547-seat Verizon Hall and the 650-seat Perleman Theater. Free tours of the building are held at 1pm daily.

Check online to find out about its 90-minute art and architecture tours held on selected Saturdays. The Kimmel also manages the gorgeous baroque-style **Academy of Music** (☎215-893-1999;

### Free Concerts

Attend excellent free classical-music concerts at the Curtis Institute of Music and **Church of the Holy Trinity Rittenhouse Square** (Map p70, D3; ☎215-567-1267; www.htrit.org; 1904 Walnut St, Rittenhouse; suggested donation $10; ⏱12:30-1:30pm Wed; 🚌9, 12, 17, 21, 42, 🚊19th St).

## Rittenhouse Farmers' Market

A Saturday morning shopping ritual for the well-heeled folks who live around Rittenhouse Sq is to stop by this year-round **farmers' market** (Map p70, E3; www.farmtocity.org; Walnut St, btwn 18th & 19th Sts; ⏰10am-2pm Sat Dec-Apr, 9am-3pm Sat May-Nov; 🚌9,12, 21, 42, 🚇19th St). Along the north side of the square you'll find stalls selling fresh fruit and veggies, a wide range of breads and baked goods, pickles, preserves, flowers and even hand-painted chocolates. Between June and November there's also a market here on Tuesdays from 10am to 2pm.

www.academyofmusic.org; 240 S Broad St, Center City; Ⓢ Walnut-Locust). (☏215-893-1999; www.kimmelcenter.org; 300 S Broad St, Center City; tickets from $10; Ⓢ Walnut-Locust or Lombard-South St)

### Chris' Jazz Cafe    JAZZ

**24** ⭐ MAP P70, G3

Showcasing local talent along with national greats, this intimate space features musicians from Monday to Saturday. Sets usually kick off around 8pm, with an extra one at 11:30pm on Friday and Saturday. (☏215-568-3131; www.chrisjazzcafe.com; 1421 Sansom St, Center City; cover $10; ⏰11am-2am; Ⓢ City Hall, 15th St or Walnut-Locust)

# Shopping

### Boyd's    FASHION & ACCESSORIES

**25** 🛍 MAP P70, E3

Boyd's has been in business since 1938, initially specializing in men's clothing, but branching out into womenswear in 1990 when they moved into the original Pennsylvania Academy of Fine Arts building. It's a grand space, especially following 2018 renovations, in which to browse and buy top designer labels. (☏215-564-9000; www.boydsphila.com; 1818 Chestnut St, Rittenhouse; ⏰9:30am-6pm Mon-Sat, to 8pm Wed; 🚇19th St)

### Stadler-Khan    GIFTS & SOUVENIRS

**26** 🛍 MAP P70, E3

Easily missed is this quirky store by designer Alex Stadler, who sells his textile and clothing designs alongside a colorful mishmash of arty gifts, crafts and vintage products. You'll find everything from felt doughnuts to Lucite table lamps. (☏267-242-7154; www.stadler-kahn.com; 1724 Sansom St, Rittenhouse; ⏰11am-6pm Mon & Wed-Fri; Ⓢ City Hall & 15th St, 🚇19th St)

### Di Bruno Bros    FOOD

**27** 🛍 MAP P70, E3

If you're after some gourmet food items, this impressive grocery/deli is almost sure to have it. It stocks a mouthwatering variety of prepared items, plus canned goods, olive oils, coffee, crackers, jams, jellies and cheeses – its specialty. There's a good self-serve cafe upstairs as well, (📞215-665-9220; https://dibruno.com; 1730 Chestnut St, Rittenhouse; 🕙7am-8:30pm Mon-Fri, to 8pm Sat, to 7pm Sun; 📶; 🚇City Hall & 15th St, 🚋19th St)

### Joan Shepp    FASHION & ACCESSORIES

28 🔒 MAP P70, E2

This chic womens-wear boutique offers a role call of designers from Comme des Garçon to Rick Owens. Credit card be damned, put yourself in the hands of its capable stylists as you shop for a complete look among its clothing, shoes, jewelry and other accessories. (📞215-735-2666; www.joanshepp.com; 1811 Chestnut St, Rittenhouse; 🕙10am-6pm Mon-Sat, to 8pm Wed, noon-5pm Sun; 🚋19th St)

### Omoi Zakka Shop    STATIONERY

29 🔒 MAP P70, F5

Get your inner Japanophile on with this shop that embraces the concept of *zakka* – stocking all things that might make life a little better. Fashion items, books, housewares, stationery and more, all with a Japan-inspired eye for cuteness or good design. (📞215-545-0963; http://omoionline.com; 1608 Pine St, Rittenhouse; 🕙noon-7pm Mon, 11am-7pm Tue-Sat, noon-5pm Sun; 🚋Lombard-South St)

**Rittenhouse Farmers' Market**

# Explore ✜

# Logan Square & Fairmount

*Since it was constructed in the early 20th century, Benjamin Franklin Pkwy has been the location of many of the city's most treasured cultural institutions, including the magnificent Philadelphia Museum of Art and massive Fairmount Park, which covers over 2000 acres either side of the Schuylkill River, and is the perfect place for exercise or a picnic.*

*Set aside several days to cover this leafy part of Philadelphia. As well as the Museum of Art (p84), the fabulous Barnes Foundation (p90) should not be missed. Also spare a few hours for the fascinating Eastern State Penitentiary (p90). The zoo (p94), Please Touch Museum (p92) and Shofuso Japanese House & Garden (p93) fall on the west side of Fairmount Park. Also fun and highly educational are the Franklin Institute (p91) and the Academy of Natural Sciences (p93).*

## Getting There & Around

🚌 Useful SEPTA buses include 7, 27, 32, 33, 38, 43 and 48. The PHLASH bus also covers Benjamin Franklin Pkwy to and from Logan Sq, as well as Eastern State Penitentiary and (on a separate service) locations in west Fairmount Park.

🚃 Route 15 connects with the zoo.

🚌 Suburban station is served by SEPTA Regional Rail lines and is a short walk from Logan Sq. East Falls and Wynnefield Ave stations can be used to access Fairmount Park.

### Neighborhood Map on p88

Logan Square and City Hall (p72) F11PHOTO/SHUTTERSTOCK ©

## Top Sight 📷
# Philadelphia Museum of Art

*The city's premier cultural institution occupies a Grecian temple–like building housing a superb collection of Asian art, Renaissance masterpieces, post-impressionist works and modern pieces by Picasso, Duchamp and Matisse among others. Especially notable are galleries filled with complete architectural ensembles, including a medieval cloister, Chinese and Indian temples and a Japanese teahouse.*

⊙ MAP P88, C3

www.philamuseum.org

2600 Benjamin Franklin Pkwy, East Fairmount Park

adult/student/child $20/14/free

🕙 10am-5pm Tue, Thu, Sat & Sun, to 8:45pm Wed & Fri

🚌 32, 38, 43

## Where to Start

Climb the broad stone steps (holding fists aloft like Rocky) to the east entrance. This provides direct access to the impressive **Great Stair Hall**, above which spins Alexander Calder's mobile *Ghost*, and around which hang the 17th-century Constantine Tapestries. This entrance provides access to the 1st- and 2nd-floor galleries, while the west entrance comes in on the ground floor.

## First Floor

In the first floor's south wing, the **American Art galleries** are notable for superb works by Charles Willson Peale, Thomas Eakins, William Merritt Chase and Henry Ossawa Tanner. The north wing includes **European Art** of the mid 19th century (this is where you'll see Van Gogh's *Sunflowers*) moving through to the **Modern & Contemporary galleries** with works by the likes of Picasso, Jasper Johns, Andy Warhol and Cy Twombly. Here too is the world's largest collection of pieces by the conceptual artist Marcel Duchamp, including *Fountain*, a 1950 replica of the porcelain urinal that created such a furor in the art world when first displayed in 1917.

## Second Floor

On the 2nd floor, the south wing's **Asian Art collection** should not be skipped. Highlights include *Sunkaraku*, a ceremonial teahouse from Japan, and a Ming-dynasty reception hall from the Palace of Zhao, as well as many stunning oriental paintings, ceramics and carpets. **Room 204** contains a medieval fountain and cloisters from the Abbey of Saint-Génis-des-Fontaines. **Room 297** houses a complete Robert Adam–designed drawing room from Lansdowne House.

### ★ Top Tips

o On the first Sunday of the month and every Wednesday after 5pm, the museum has a pay-what-you-want policy.

o Your ticket, which is valid for two days, also includes entry to the Perelman Building (p94), which hosts good rotating exhibits devoted to photography, fashion, art and design; and the Rodin Museum (p92), housing a superb collection of works by the French sculptor Auguste Rodin.

### ✕ Take a Break

There are several places to eat and drink in the museum, including a couple of cafes and a new **restaurant** that's part of the Frank Gehry upgrade.

Cycling Tour

# Fairmount Park Pedal

*This tour of Philly's central green lung follows part of the Schuylkill River Trail (https://schuylkill rivertrail.com) cycling paths on the east and west banks of the river. However, if you don't fancy cycling it's possible to walk or drive the route and see several of the sights along the way.*

## Route Facts

**Start** Boathouse Row; 32, 38

**End** East Falls train station; East Falls

**Length** 4 miles; three to four hours

# ❶ Boathouse Row

This picturesque strip of **rowing clubs** (☎215-685-3936; www.boat houserow.org; 1 Boathouse Row; ☒32, 38) is made up of mock Tudor and Victorian boathouses from the late 19th and early 20th centuries. Check the website for the racing schedule between each of the mainly university clubs.

# ❷ Lemon Hill

This 1799 **mansion** (☎215-232-4337; http://parkcharms.com/lemon-hill; Lemon Hill Dr; adult/student/child $8/5/free; ☻10am-4pm Apr–mid-Dec; ☒38), one of several preserved within Fairmount Park, is named after the lemon trees that once grew in the greenhouses that were on the estate in the early 19th century.

# ❸ Ellen Phillips Samuel Memorial

This riverside garden section of the **park** (www.associationforpublic art.org/artwork/ellen-phillips-samuel-memorial; Kelly Dr; ☒W Girard Ave & 33rd St) comprises three terraces decorated with 17 sculptures that were commissioned between 1933 and 1961.

# ❹ Historic Strawberry Mansion

Fairmount Park's largest historic **mansion** (☎215-228-8364; www. historicstrawberrymansion.org; 2450 Strawberry Mansion Dr; adult/student/child $8/5/free; ☻10am-4pm

Tue-Sun Apr-Dec; ☒32) combines Federal-style and Greek Revival architecture. It's home to some fine antiques and art, including porcelain, furniture and Victorian dolls.

# ❺ Laurel Hill Cemetery

For those interested in landscape gardening this **burial ground** (☎215-228-8200; https://thelaurel hillcemetery.org; 3822 Ridge Ave; tours $12-40; ☻8am-4:30pm Mon-Fri, from 9:30am Sat & Sun; ☒61), founded in 1836, is famous and worth exploring. Numerous prominent Philadelphians are buried here, including David Rittenhouse and Frank Furness.

# ❻ Trolley Car Cafe

The old brick building is home to this pleasant **cafe** (☎267-385-6703; http://trolleycarcafe.com; 3269 S Ferry Rd, East Falls; mains $10-12; ☻7am-3pm; ☒East Falls) with outdoor seating overlooking the Schuylkill River. Some of the ingredients used in the cafe's salads and sandwiches are grown at an on-site garden.

## ✕ Bike Rental

Rent from **Wheel Fun Rentals** (Map p88, B2; ☎215-232-7778; https://wheelfunrentals.com/; 1 Boathouse Row; hr/half-/full day from $10/25/32; ☻10am-sunset Apri–mid-May, from 9am mid-May–mid-Nov; ☒32) near the start of the circuit.

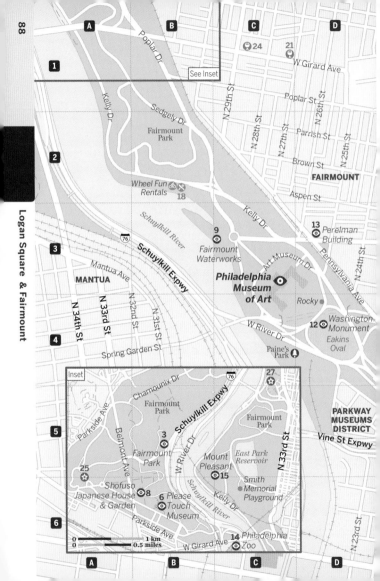

Logan Square & Fairmount

N College Ave

Girard College

S College Ave

W Girard Ave

W Thompson St

N 18th St
N 17th St
N 16th St
N 15th St

Ridge Ave

Poplar St

Poplar St

N 19th St

N 20th St

Corinthian Ave

N 22nd St
N 23rd St

Parrish St

Philadelphia
Metropolitan
Opera House

Brown St

Eastern State
Penitentiary
**2** ◉

Francis St

Brown St

Fairmount Ave

Fairmount Ⓜ

**23** 🍴    🔒 **28**

Ⓠ **20**

North St

Wallace St

Mt Vernon St

Green St

N 21st St
N 22nd St
N 23rd St

Brandywine St

🔒 **29**

N 19th St

N 18th St

Mt Vernon St

N 17th St
N 16th St

**26** ✪

Broad St

Spring Garden St

N 20th St

Spring Garden Ⓜ
(Broad St Line)

**16** ✕

Rodin
Museum
◉ **7**

Hamilton St

21st St

Benjamin Franklin Pkwy

**17** ✕

Barnes
Foundation
◉ **1**

Ⓠ ✕
**22  19**

Callowhill St

**5** ◉ Parkway Central
Library

Vine St

Vine St Expwy

Winter St

Franklin
Institute
◉ **4**

N 22nd St

Race St

Logan Circle
& Square

**10** Cathedral
◉ Basilica of Saints
Peter and Paul

Academy of
Natural Sciences ◉
**11**

Cherry St

N 21st St
N 20th St
N 19th St

N 18th St

Arch St

Benjamin Franklin Pkwy

N 16th St

**For reviews see**
◉ Top Sights      p84
◉ Sights          p90
✕ Eating          p95
Ⓠ Drinking        p96
✪ Entertainment   p98
🔒 Shopping        p99

N
0        500 m
0        0.25 miles

E    F    G    H

1

2

3

4

5

6

# Sights

## Barnes Foundation    MUSEUM

1  MAP P88, E5

In the first half of the 20th century, collector and educator Albert C Barnes amassed a remarkable trove of artwork by Cézanne, Degas, Matisse, Renoir, Van Gogh and other European stars. Alongside, he set beautiful pieces of folk art from Africa and the Americas – an artistic desegregation that was shocking at the time. Today's Barnes Foundation is a contemporary shell, inside which is a faithful reproduction of the galleries of Barnes' original mansion (still in the Philadelphia suburbs).

The art is hung according to Barnes' vision, a careful juxtaposition of colors, themes and materials. In one room, all the portraits appear to be staring at a central point. Even more remarkable: you've likely never seen any of these works before, because Barnes' will limits reproduction and lending.

The first Sunday of the month admission is free. Tickets are limited to four per person and there's a focus on family activities. (☎215-278-7200; www.barnesfoundation.org; 2025 Benjamin Franklin Pkwy, Spring Garden; adult/student/child $25/5/free; ⏱10am-5pm Wed-Mon; 🚌7, 32, 33, 38, 48)

## Eastern State Penitentiary    MUSEUM

2  MAP P88, E3

The modern prison didn't just happen – it was invented, and Eastern State Penitentiary was the first one, opened in 1829 and finally closed in 1971. A self-guided audio tour leads you through the eerie, echoing halls; one stop is Al Capone's famously luxurious cell. There's also info on America's current prison system, and art installations throughout. A popular stop, expect crowds at peak times.

From mid-September through Halloween, the prison hosts a truly terrifying haunted house. (☎215-236-3300; www.easternstate.org; 2027 Fairmount Ave, Fairmount; adult/child $14/10; ⏱10am-5pm; 🚌48, 43, 33)

## Fairmount Park    PARK

3  MAP P88, B5

The snaking Schuylkill River bisects this 2050-acre green space,

---

### Rocky Statue    📷

A major Philly selfie spot is this 1980 work by A Thomas Schomberg of the fictional boxer **Rocky** (Map p88, D4; www.associationforpublicart.org/artwork/rocky; 2600 Benjamin Franklin Pkwy, Fairmount; 🚌32, 38, 43) from the 1976 Oscar-winner *Rocky*. The statue was created for a scene in Rocky III and had various locations around town before ending up back in its spiritual home here next to the Museum of Art steps in 2006.

the largest city park in the US, splitting it into east and west sections. On either side of the river are cycling and jogging paths, playing fields, lawns, public art and several historic mansions. (https://myphilly park.org; admission free; 🚇32, 38)

## Franklin Institute           MUSEUM

4 ⊙ MAP P88, E6

You could easily spend the better part of the day touring this world-class science museum. As well as being the venue for temporary blockbuster science exhibitions, there's a planetarium, IMAX cinema and great permanent features such as a giant two-story replica of a beating heart where kids can crawl through the arteries.

The institute was founded in 1824 by Benjamin Franklin; a memorial to him in the lobby includes a stunning 20ft-high marble statue in a rotunda modeled after the Pantheon in Rome.The museum hosts much of the **Philadelphia Science Festival** (www.phila sciencefestival.org) each April. (📞215-448-1200; www.fi.edu; 222 N 20th St, Logan Sq; adult/child $23/19, special exhibits extra; ⏱9:30am-5pm; 🚇33, 38, 48)

## Parkway Central Library           LIBRARY

5 ⊙ MAP P88, F5

Worth visiting for its splendid architecture, this main branch of the Free Library of Philadelphia has free tours at 10am on Tuesday, Thursday, Saturday and the first Sunday of the month, and at 2pm

Statue of Benjamin Franklin, Franklin Institute

## Upgrading the Philadelphia Museum of Art

A $196-million program is underway to rejuvenate the **Philadelphia Museum of Art** (p84) and prepare it for the coming decades. In what is called the Core Project, architect Frank Gehry is creating new galleries and common areas, adding 67,000 sq ft of public space to the museum and helping to improve navigation and circulation for visitors.

The new central Forum will provide a connecting space and clear views between Lenfest Hall at the western entrance and the Great Stairs Hall at the eastern entrance. The north entrance, closed since 1975, will be reopened and connected to the Forum. A north–south Vaulted Walkway, long closed off, will also be publicly accessible. All this work should be completed by 2020. Plans and a scale model for the upgrade can be seen in **Room 154** of the main building.

on Monday, Wednesday, Friday and Saturday. From Monday to Saturday there's a tour at 11am of the Rare Book Department, with its collection of works and manuscripts relating to Charles Dickens, Edgar Allan Poe and Americana. (☎215-686-5322; www.freelibrary.org; 1901 Vine St, Spring Garden; admission free; ☉9am-9pm Mon-Thu, to 6pm Fri, to 5pm Sat, 1-5pm Sun; 🚍27, 32, 33, 38)

### Please Touch Museum
MUSEUM

6 ◉ MAP P88, B6

Parents will have a lot of fun at what's definitely a kiddo goldmine: splash around learning about bubbles, race toy cars, wander through a 'wonderland' of trick mirrors and illusions, ride a beautiful antique fairground carousel.

Memorial Hall is where the 1876 Centennial Exposition was held and is one of the few remaining buildings in the park from that event. Its basement houses a scale-model of the Exposition. Tickets are available to see the model. (☎215-581-3181; www.pleasetouchmuseum.org; 4231 Ave of the Republic, West Fairmount Park; admission $19; ☉9am-5pm Mon-Sat, 11am-5pm Sun; 🚍38)

### Rodin Museum
MUSEUM

7 ◉ MAP P88, E5

This is the only institution outside of Paris dedicated to the French sculptor Auguste Rodin. The superb collection is based on works amassed by Jules E Mastbaum in the 1920s. There are versions of *The Thinker* and *Burghers of Calais* among its 140 sculptures spanning every part of Rodin's spectacular career. (☎215-763-8100; www.rodinmuseum.org; 2151 Benjamin Franklin Pkwy, Spring Garden; suggested donation $10; ☉10am-5pm Wed-Mon; 🚍7, 32, 33, 38, 48)

## Shofuso Japanese House & Garden

GARDENS

**8** ◉ MAP P88, B6

This picturesque house, built in Nagoya in 1953 to a 17th-century design, has been set in 1.2 acres of traditional Japanese gardens in Fairmount Park since 1958. Check online for various events, including tea ceremonies, that are held here (bookings and extra payment required). The cherry trees blooming in spring are not to be missed (☎215-878-5097; www.japanese house.org; Horticultural Dr, West Fairmount Park; adult/child $12/8; ⏰10am-4pm Wed-Fri, 11am-7pm Sat & Sun Apr-Oct; 🚌38)

## Fairmount Waterworks

MUSEUM

**9** ◉ MAP P88, C3

A National Historic Engineering Landmark, this beautiful Greek Revival complex was built in 1815 and pumped water from the Schuylkill River for the city's consumption until 1909. It was one of Philadelphia's biggest tourist attractions in its day and is still well worth a visit for its excellent interpretative center, where you can learn about the pumping station's history, the area's natural history, and conservation of water resources and the environment. (☎215-685-0723; http://fairmountwaterworks.org; 640 Waterworks Dr, East Fairmount Park; admission by donation, tours $10; ⏰10am-5pm Tue-Sat, 1-5pm Sun; 🚌32, 38)

## Cathedral Basilica of Saints Peter and Paul

CATHEDRAL

**10** ◉ MAP P88, F6

The focus of Catholic life in Philadelphia is this gorgeously decorated cathedral, dedicated in 1864 and enlarged in 1957. The oldest building on Logan Sq, it was designed by Napoleon LeBrun and John Notman and includes a copper covered dome and Palladian facade. The interior dazzles with its murals, mosaics and stained glass. (☎215-561-1313; http://cathedralphila.org; 1723 Race St, Logan Sq; admission free; ⏰9am-5pm; 🚌27, 32, 33)

## Academy of Natural Sciences

MUSEUM

**11** ◉ MAP P88, F6

You'll find plenty of kid-pleasing exhibits at the country's oldest natural-history museum, including a hot and humid butterfly room with live specimens, and a terrific dinosaur exhibition where you can dig for fossils and bones. You can also watch scientists extracting fossils from surrounding stone. (☎215-299-1019; www.ansp.org; 1900 Benjamin Franklin Pkwy, Logan Sq; adult/child $19.95/15.95; ⏰10am-4:30pm Mon-Fri, to 5pm Sat & Sun; 🚌32, 33, 38)

## Washington Monument

FOUNTAIN

**12** ◉ MAP P88, D4

Rudolf Siemering's 1897 monument to General George

## Skateboarding Park 👍

Philadelphia is a national leader for skateboarding culture. Riverside **Paine's Park** (Map p88, C4; http://franklinspaine.com/skateparks/paines-park; off Martin Luther King Jr Dr, Fairmount; admission free; ⏰6am-10pm; 🚌32, 38), designed specifically for boarders, is the first of several that a non-profit group hopes to build around the city.

Washington is a marvelous ensemble. Proudly mounted astride his horse, the first US president sits atop a band of allegorical figures and is surrounded at the monument's base by American flora and fauna with figures that include equally proud looking Native Americans. (www.associationforpublicart.org/artwork/washington-monument; Eakins Oval, Fairmount; admission free; 🚌32, 38, 43)

## Perelman Building   MUSEUM

13 ◎ MAP P88, D3

This fine art-deco building, a branch of the Philadelphia Museum of Art, houses small galleries devoted to special exhibitions of costumes, textiles, prints, drawings, photographs, and modern and contemporary design.

Known as 'the Gateway to Fairmount Park' when it opened in 1927, the building was originally offices for the Fidelity Mutual Life Insurance Company. It has an elaborately sculpted facade decorated with Egyptian-inspired reliefs. (📞215-763-8100; www.philamuseum.org; 2525 Pennsylvania Ave, Fairmount; incl in admission to Philadelphia Museum of Art adult/student/child \$20/14/free; ⏰10am-5pm Tue-Sun; 🚌32, 38, 43)

## Philadelphia Zoo   ZOO

14 ◎ MAP P88, C6

The country's oldest zoo (first opened in 1874) is home to nearly 1300 animals including tigers, pumas, polar bears – you name it – in naturalistic habitats. Its unique Zoo360 series of see-through mesh trails for gorillas, big apes, tigers and meerkats, allow these animals more space to roam the zoo grounds. (📞215-243-1100; www.philadelphiazoo.org; 3400 W Girard Ave, West Fairmount Park; adult/child \$25/20; ⏰9:30am-5pm Mar-Oct, to 4pm Nov-Feb; 🚌38)

## Mount Pleasant   HISTORIC BUILDING

15 ◎ MAP P88, C5

This 1764 mansion was described by John Adams in 1775 'as the most elegant seat in Pennsylvania.' The Georgian building is closed for general maintenance, but its lovely Georgian exterior and flanking outbuildings still have bags of visual appeal. (www.philamuseum.org; 3800 Mt Pleasant Dr, East Fairmount Park; ⏰closed to public; 🚌W Girard Ave & 33rd St)

# Eating

## Whole Foods Market FOOD HALL $

16 🅢 MAP P88, E4

Apart from being an excellent grocery store with plenty of prepared food to go, this flagship branch of Whole Foods includes a superb food court with stalls run by Federal Donuts, Dizengoff (for creamy hummus and Israeli salads), Goldie (for falafel), Genji Izakaya (for Japanese bites) and Whiz Kid (for vegan cheesesteaks).

Allegro Coffee provides hot beverages, while the Parkway Pub serves plenty of local beers on tap as well as other alcoholic drinks. (☎215-557-0015; www.wholefoods market.com; 2101 Pennsylvania Ave, Spring Garden; mains $7-10; ⏰7am-11pm; 🚇7, 32, 33, 38, 48)

## Garden Restaurant INTERNATIONAL $$

17 🅢 MAP P88, E5

The Star Catering Group bring its usual professional touch to this appealing restaurant in the Barnes Foundation. There's a lovely garden view through floor-to-ceiling windows and a menu that plays it safe with dishes such as lox and dill toast, grilled organic chicken, falafel and generous salads. (☎215-278-7070; www.barnesfounda tion.org; 2025 Benjamin Franklin Pkwy, Spring Garden; mains $13-20; ⏰11:30am-3:30pm Mon & Wed-Fri, 11am-4pm Sat & Sun; 🛜; 🚇7, 32, 33)

Whole Foods Market

JOHN GREIM/GETTY IMAGES ©

## Wissahickon Valley Park

Covering 2042 acres, this beautiful, wooded **park** (www.fow.org; Valley Green Rd) follows the Wissahickon Creek from its confluence with the Schuylkill River up to the city's northwest boundary. With vehicle access to the park mostly banned it's a wonderful spot for hiking, mountain biking or horseback riding.

If you're coming by train, Wissahickon is the station closest to the southern end of the park, while Tulpehocken is not far east of the location of the **Historic Rittenhouse Town** (☏ 215-438-5711; https://rittenhousetown.org; 208 Lincoln Dr; adult/child $5/2.50; ◷ 1-5pm Sat & Sun early Jun–end Sep; ☒ Tulpehocken) where the first paper mill in North America was established in the late 17th century. Alternatively, drive into the park along Valley Green Rd and park next to the **Valley Green Inn** (☏ 215-247-1730; www.valleygreeninn.com; mains $14-29; ◷ noon-3pm & 4-8pm Nov-Apr, noon-4pm & 5-10pm May-Oct; ☒ St Martins). The welcome couldn't be warmer at this idyllic creekside inn that dates back to the 1850s and appears little changed since then. The menu is stacked with classic American comfort food.

## Cosmic Cafe at Lloyd Hall

CAFE $

18 ⊗ MAP P88, B2

Where possible this Fairmount Park cafe cooks with ingredients from local farmers using sustainable farming practices. The location by the river and picturesque Boathouse Row makes it a lovely spot for a coffee and a sandwich. (☏ 215-978-0900; http://cosmicfoods.com; 1 Boathouse Row, East Fairmount Park; sandwiches $8-14; ◷ 8am-8pm; ⧈; ☒ 32)

## Sabrina's Cafe

AMERICAN $

19 ⊗ MAP P88, F5

This branch of the popular brunch cafe serves its filling egg, salad and comfort food dishes all the way through to dinner.

The original Sabrina's is near the **Italian Market** (☏ 215-574-1599; 910 Christian St, Bella Vista; breakfast $10-14; ◷ 8am-5pm; ⧈ ⧈; ☒ 47, Ⓢ Ellsworth-Federal). (☏ 215-636-9061; www.sabrinascafe.com; 1804 Callowhill St, Spring Garden; breakfast $10-14; ◷ 8am-10pm Tue-Sat, to 4pm Sun & Mon)

# Drinking

## Bar Hygge

MICROBREWERY

20 ☺ MAP P88, G3

Pronounced 'Hug-uh,' Hygge has a weekend brunch that can't be beat, but the real gems are its house-made Techne draft beers, which include English-style ales,

IPAs and porters: all are excellent. The walls are made of cut-up pieces of wine barrels, making for interesting, artsy ambience. (📞215-765-2274; www.barhygge.com; 1720 Fairmount Ave, Fairmount; craft cocktails $10; 🕐4-11pm Mon-Fri, from 10:30am Sat & Sun; **S**Fairmount)

### Crime & Punishment Brewing Co
MICROBREWERY

21 🔵 MAP P88, C1

It's rare to come across a craft-beer brewery that celebrates Russian literature, but such is Crime & Punishment, where the ales are anything but hard labor. There are some unique and tasty beers to sample including their flagship IPA Space Race and the Polish sour-style Grod Inquisitor.

Keeping with the Eastern European theme are snacks such as pierogi and Kielbasa sausage sandwiches. The bar also acts as a gallery space with new exhibitions opening on the first Friday of each month. (📞215-235-2739; http://crimeandpunishmentbrewingco.com; 2711 W Girard Ave, Brewerytown; 🕐4pm-midnight Mon-Wed, to 1am Fri, 11-1am Sat, 11am-midnight Sun; 🛜; 🚋W Girard Ave & 27th St)

### Kite & Key
PUB

22 🔵 MAP P88, F5

Handy for refreshments if you're near the city end of Ben Franklin Pkwy, this convivial pub has a fine selection of craft beers on tap, a good menu that includes flatbreads and mussels, and outdoor drinking and dining areas for when the weather is warm. (📞215-568-1818; www.thekiteandkey.com; 1836 Callowhill St, Spring Garden; 🕐11am-2am)

### OCF Coffee House
CAFE

23 🔵 MAP P88, E3

This chain cafe serving La Columbe coffee and a tasty selection of snacks pops up where its owners, a real-estate development company, has projects. This branch is large, with a sparse

### Smith Memorial Playground

A boon to parents seeking to entertain kids of 10 years or younger is the **Smith Memorial Playground** (Map p88, C6; 📞215-765-4325; http://smithplayground.org; 3500 Reservoir Dr, East Fairmount Park; 🕐10am-4pm Tue-Sun Oct-Mar; 10am-6pm Tue-Fri, to 7pm Sat & Sun Apr-Sep; 🚌32). The 6.5-acre playground includes a giant wooden slide, swings, a giant net climber and many other pieces of play equipment. In the Playhouse, children aged five and younger can take part in activities such as riding a train, messing around in a room full of kid-sized cars and tricycles with real traffic lights, and playing with puppets.

## Metropolitan Opera House ⓘ

This grand old **dame** (Map p88, H2; 858 N Broad St, Francisville; **S**Fairmount), on the National Register of Historic Places, was designed by William H McElfatrick and used by various opera companies through the 1930s. Once the largest theater of its kind in the world, it has sat largely empty and unloved for years. A major restoration by Live Nation will see it reopen as a 4000-seat venue by the end of 2018.

industrial interior and plenty of natural light. (☏267-773-8081; www. ocfrealty.com/coffee-house; 2100 Fairmount Ave, Fairmount; ⏱6:30am-8pm Mon-Fri, from 7:30am Sat & Sun; 🛜; 🚌48, 43, 33, 32, 7)

### The Monkey & The Elephant
CAFE

24 🚇 MAP P88, C1

Youths who were once part of the foster-home system in Philly are provided with work and other life skills at this appealing non-profit cafe. It serves all the usual drinks plus house-made baked goods and paninis. Locally-sourced crafts and food products are sold here, and there's a pleasant courtyard out the back. (☏267-457-5334; www. themonkeyandtheelephant.org; 2831 W Girard Ave, Brewerytown; ⏱7am-11am Mon, to 7pm Tue-Sun; 🚋W Girard Ave, 28th or 29th Sts)

# Entertainment

## Mann Center
LIVE MUSIC

25 ⭐ MAP P88, A5

Major stars including Smokey Robinson, Aretha Franklin, Ryan Adams and Sigur Rós, have played this superb outdoor arena on a hill overlooking Fairmount Park and the city skyline. The Philadelphia Orchestra also plays concerts here. As well as the main stage, there's also the Skyline Stage, a standing-room-only venue. (☏215-546-7900; https://manncenter.org; 5201 Parkside Ave, West Fairmount Park; tickets from $50; ⏱May-Sep; 🚌Mann Center Loop bus to Crawford Circle)

## South
LIVE MUSIC

26 ⭐ MAP P88, H4

Doors for the jazz parlor at this Southern-food restaurant and bar open at 6pm, and you're advised to get here early as it's general seating and very popular. Shows usually kick off at 7pm – check online for a full schedule and note some performances are ticketed. (☏215-600-0220; https://southjazz kitchen.com/; 600 N Broad St, Spring Garden; tickets from $25; ⏱4-10pm Tue-Sun; **S**Spring Garden)

## Dell East Music Center
LIVE MUSIC

27 ⭐ MAP P88, C4

Check to see who is playing at this large outdoor amphitheater during its summer season of popular music concerts, which also include some classical performances by the Black Pearl Chamber Orchestra (www.blackpearlco.org) and dance performances by PHILADANCO (www.philadanco.org). (📞215-685-9560; www.mydelleast.com; 2400 Strawberry Mansion Dr, East Fairmount Park; 🕐Jun-Sep; 🚌32)

# Shopping

## Neighborhood Potters

ARTS & CRAFTS

28 🔒 MAP P88, F3

Sandi and Neil are the couple behind this creative pottery studio and gallery, which opens its doors to shoppers for a few hours each weekend if it doesn't have an exhibition on (when it keeps longer hours). You can also take pottery classes here. (📞215-236-1617; www.sandiandneil.com; 2034 Fairmount Ave, Fairmount; 🕐noon-4pm Sat; 🚌48, 43, 33, 32, 7)

## Old Philly Ale House

ALCOHOL

29 🔒 MAP P88, F4

Choose from hundreds of different beers, local and international, regular or exotic, at this shop, which also hosts weekly tastings of different ales. (📞215-563-1665; www.oldphillyalehouse.com; 565 N 20th St, Spring Gardens; 🕐11am-midnight Sun-Thu, to 1am Fri & Sat; 🚌33)

Aretha Franklin performing at the Mann Center

# Walking Tour 🥾

# Down Manayunk's Main St

*A Native American word meaning 'where we go to drink', Manayunk remains a fine location in which to undertake this activity. All kinds of beverages are available along Main St, the attractive commercial strip lined with renovated Victorian storefronts and mill buildings at the foot of steep residential streets. There's also a canal you can cycle beside.*

## Getting There

🚆 Suburban trains run each hour ($5.25; 20 minutes) between Manayunk and downtown Philadelphia.

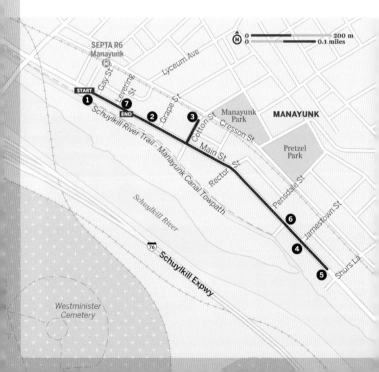

### ❶ Manayunk Canal

The **towpath** (www.manayunkcanal. org) along the Manayunk Canal has been revived as part of the Schuylkill River Trail. Look out for the wall mosaics of the birds of Fairmount Park and for the nine mosaic-covered steps that make up Diane Pieri's artwork celebrating the area's flora, fauna and industrial heritage.

### ❷ Pineapple on Main

Main St is stacked with independent retailers such as this **one** (☏267-437-4014; www.pineappleon main.com; 4347 Main St; ⏰11am-7pm Tue-Thu, to 8pm Fri & Sat, 10am-5pm Sat), stocking home decor, babywear, stationery and bath and body products, with many sourced from local artisans.

### ❸ Spiral Bookcase

Just off Main St is this cute, proactive indie **bookstore** (☏215-482-0704; http://thespiralbookcase.com; 112 Cotton St; ⏰noon-5pm Mon, to 8pm Tue-Fri, 11am-8pm Sat, 11am-6pm Sun) where book launches are occasionally held and some unusual publications are recommended.

### ❹ Pilgrim Roasters

Perk yourself up with Pilgrim's small-batch **coffees** (☏267-331-5213; www.pilgrimroasters.com; 4120 Main St; ⏰6am-6pm Mon-Fri, 7am-7pm Sat, 8am-5pm Sun; 🛜), all single origin and with different flavor profiles. A Scandinavian light roasting technique is used to avoid any bitter taste from the beans.

### ❺ Manayunk Brewing Company

This **brewery** (☏215-482-8220; www.manayunkbrewery.com; 4120 Main St; ⏰11am-11pm Mon-Thu, until 2am Fri & Sat, 10:30am-10pm Sun) has been making craft beer since 1996. Flights go for $11 and can be enjoyed in a lively beer hall. There's also live jazz on Tuesday nights and for Sunday brunch.

### ❻ Trek Bicycle Philadelphia Manayunk

Buy or rent a bicycle **here** (☏215-487-7433; www.trekbikes.com/us/ en_US/retail/philadelphia_manayunk; 4159 Main St; per hr/day from $15/60; ⏰10am-7pm Mon-Fri, to 6pm Sat, 11am-5pm Sun) for a longer pedal along the canal towpath. Or you could take on the notorious Manayunk Wall, an 800m climb up nearby Levering St and Lyceum Ave that has a 17% grade at its steepest.

### ❼ Tubby Robot

Treat yourself to a scoop from **Tubby Robot** (☏267-423-4376; www.tubbyrobot.com; 4369 Main St; one scoop $4; ⏰noon-9pm Thu-Sun), where the ices are all handmade with fresh ingredients. Video arcade games from the 1980s and '90s are a nice retro touch.

# Explore
# Fishtown &
# Northern Liberties

*The gentrification that started a couple of decades ago in the former manufacturing district of Northern Liberties ('NoLibs') has since spread to Fishtown (so called because this was where the city's fishing industry was once based) and parts of Kensington. While these areas are light on traditional sights they are increasingly popular spots to eat, drink, party and shop.*

*The area was once strongly working class with several breweries. Such businesses are making a comeback, supplemented by spirits distilleries and the studios of artists and craftspeople. The key sights are the first phase of the Rail Park (p106) and the nearby Rodeph Shalom Synagogue (p106). Head here on a weekend to access the Edgar Allan Poe National Historic Site (p106), where the writer once lived; this is also a good time to check out what's happening in gallery spaces such as Crane Arts (p106).*

## Getting There & Around

🚌 SEPTA buses 43 and 61 go along Spring Garden St; 5 and 25 are also useful for traveling north–south routes.

Ⓢ Useful Market-Frankford Line subway stations include Spring Garden, Girard, Berks and York-Dauphin. On the Broad Street Line there are also separate Spring Garden and Girard stations.

🚃 Trolley services (sometimes replaced by buses) run along Girard St from Frankford and Delaware.

### Neighborhood Map on p104

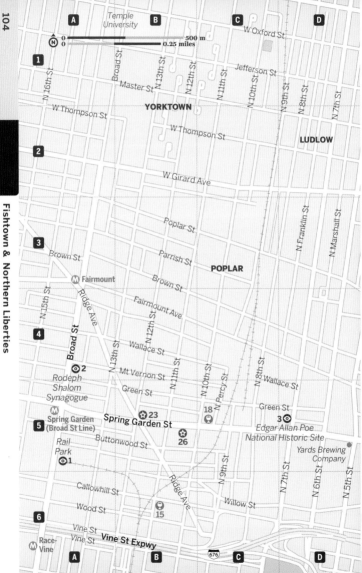

A B C D

Temple University

0 ———— 500 m
0 ———— 0.25 miles

W Oxford St

Jefferson St

**1**

N 16th St
Broad St
N 13th St
N 12th St
N 11th St
N 10th St
N 9th St
N 8th St
N 7th St

Master St

**YORKTOWN**

W Thompson St

W Thompson St

**LUDLOW**

**2**

W Girard Ave

Poplar St

Parrish St

N Franklin St
N Marshall St

**3**

Brown St

**POPLAR**

Ⓜ Fairmount

Ridge Ave

Brown St

Fairmount Ave

**4**

N 15th St
Broad St
N 13th St
N 12th St
Wallace St
N 11th St
Mt Vernon St
N 10th St
N Percy St
N 9th St
N 8th St

Wallace St

◉ 2
Rodeph
Shalom
Synagogue

Green St

Green St

3 ◉

Ⓜ Spring Garden
(Broad St Line)
**5**

Spring Garden St
✪ 23

18
Ⓢ

Edgar Allan Poe
National Historic Site

Buttonwood St

✪
26

Yards Brewing
Company

Rail
Park
◉ 1

Callowhill St

Ridge Ave

Willow St

N 9th St
N 7th St
N 6th St
N 5th St

**6**

Wood St

Ⓢ
15

Vine St
Vine St
Ⓜ Race-
Vine

**Vine St Expwy**

676

A B C D

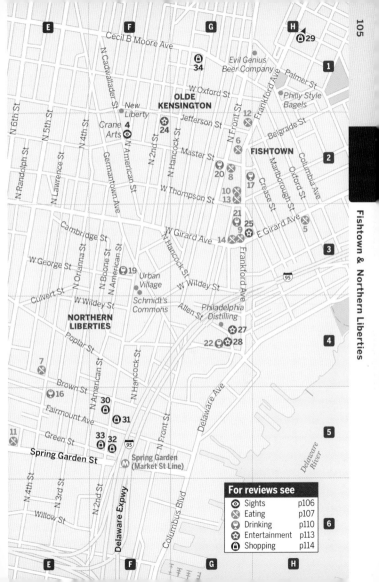

Cecil B Moore Ave

Evil Genius
Beer Company

Palmer St

Philly Style
Bagels

**OLDE
KENSINGTON**

W Oxford St

Jefferson St

**FISHTOWN**

New
Liberty

Crane
Arts

Master St

N Cadwalader St

N 6th St

N 5th St

N 4th St

N Randolph St

N Lawrence St

Germantown Ave

N American St

N 2nd St

N Hancock St

N Front St

Frankford Ave

Belgrade St

Columbia Ave

Oxford St

Marlborough St

Crease St

W Thompson St

Cambridge St

W George St

Culvert St

W Wildey St

**NORTHERN
LIBERTIES**

Poplar St

Brown St

Fairmount Ave

Green St

Spring Garden St

Willow St

N Orianna St

N Boone St

N American St

N Hancock St

Urban
Village

Schmidt's
Commons

Allen St

W Wildey St

W Girard Ave

E Girard Ave

Philadelphia
Distilling

Frankford Ave

N Front St

Delaware Ave

Delaware Expwy

Spring Garden
(Market St Line)

Columbus Blvd

Delaware River

**Fishtown & Northern Liberties**

| For reviews see | |
|---|---|
| ⊙ Sights | p106 |
| ✕ Eating | p107 |
| 🍷 Drinking | p110 |
| ★ Entertainment | p113 |
| 🅐 Shopping | p114 |

# Sights

## Rail Park
PARK

1 ◉ MAP P104, A5

The old Reading Viaduct is the location of the first phase of this ambitious project to reuse 3 miles of decommissioned rail lines between Fairmount Park and Center City. A bridge over N 13th St has been rebuilt, old rail girders have been incorporated into planters and quotes in different languages are carved into paving stones.

Swing seats on the viaduct section of the park provide great views of Shepard Fairey's mural **The Stamp of Incarceration** (www.muralarts.org/artworks/open-source/the-stamp-of-incarceration/). Look also for an old train dining car parked at the Broad St end of the park, which is set to be turned into a visitors' center. (https://therailpark.org; Broad & Noble Sts, Callowhill; ⓢ Spring Garden: Broad St Line)

## Rodeph Shalom Synagogue
SYNAGOGUE

2 ◉ MAP P104, A4

Home to the oldest Jewish Ashkenazi congregation in the US, Rodeph Shalom is one of the most beautiful pieces of religious architecture in Philadelphia. The 1927 building, designed by Simon & Simon, features Babylonian and Assyrian patterns on its exterior, while the spectacular domed interior is a riot of stenciled mosaics, gilt and stained glass with Byzantine and Moorish allusions.

Historians bemoan the fact that a Frank Furness–designed synagogue was torn down in the 1920s to create this building. Photos of the Furness building hang in the synagogue's contemporary main entrance, added in 2015, which also includes an interesting Museum of Jewish Art. (☏ 215-627-6747; https://rodephshalom.org; 615 N Broad St, Poplar; donation $5; ⊙ by appointment; ⓢ Spring Garden: Broad Street Line)

## Edgar Allan Poe National Historic Site
HISTORIC SITE

3 ◉ MAP P104, D5

Often called the creator of the horror story, Edgar Allan Poe lived for six years in Philadelphia, in five different houses. This historic site, his only Philly home still remaining, is now a small but interesting museum, with a lot of original items and restored rooms. Don't miss the creepy brick cellar (complete with cobwebs) thought to have inspired Poe's masterwork *The Black Cat*. A statue of a raven stands outside. (☏ 215-597-8780; www.nps.gov/edal; 532 N 7th St, Poplar; admission free; ⊙ 9am-5pm Fri-Sun; ⓢ Spring Garden: Market-Frankford Line)

## Crane Arts
ARTS CENTER

4 ◉ MAP P104, F2

As well as the several art galleries and artist studios that occupy this former plumbing supplies warehouse, you'll find the Icebox Project Space (Thursday to Saturday), which is sometimes used for performance art and theatrical works, and the Philadelphia Photo Arts Center (www.philaphotoarts.org), which mounts regular exhibitions and hosts workshops. (☎215-232-3203; www.cranearts.com; 1400 N American St, Kensington; admission free; ⊗most galleries noon-6pm Wed-Sat; ⑤Girard: Market-Frankford Line)

# Eating

## Stock
SOUTHEAST ASIAN $$

5 ✕ MAP P104, H3

At this no-frills BYOB it's all about the taste of the food – which is delicious and authentic. Piquant salads, such as the Burmese gin thoke or Vietnamese-style green papaya, come piled high, while steaming large bowls of noodles are lovingly made and packed with flavor. (☎302-559-4872; www.stockphilly.com; 308 E Girard Ave, Fishtown; ⚲; ⑤Girard: Market-Frankford Line)

## CHeU Fishtown
ASIAN $$

6 ✕ MAP P104, G2

Asian buns, dumplings and noodles with a Jewish mama's twist (smoked matzo balls and brisket in the ramen, for example) have made CHeU a hit. The fusion dishes taste great and the funky diner-meets-punk-street-art feel of the place is appealing. (☎267-758-2269; www.cheufishtown.com; 1416 Frankford Ave, Fishtown; noodles $12-14; ⊗noon-3pm & 5-10pm Mon-Thu, to 11pm Fri, noon-11pm Sat, noon-10pm Sun; ⑤Girard: Market-Frankford Line)

Rodeph Shalom Synagogue

B O KANE/ALAMY STOCK PHOTO ©

## North Central Philadelphia

Home to the campus of Temple University (www.temple.edu), North Central Philadelphia is a largely African American neighborhood that is worth a visit for a couple of outstanding sights.

The extraordinary **Wagner Free Institute of Science** (☎215-763-6529; www.wagnerfreeinstitute.org; 1700 W Montgomery Ave,; suggested donation adult/child $10/5; ⏰9am-4pm Tue-Fri; Ⓢ Cecil B Moore) is home to over 100,000 natural-history specimens. All have been preserved just as they were presented in the 1890s by the museum's founder William Wagner. No photos are allowed but drawing is encouraged, and there's a packed schedule of evening lectures and family-friendly weekend programs.

Call ahead to arrange a visit to the extraordinary **Church of the Advocate** (☎215-978-8008; www.churchoftheadvocate.org; 1801 W Diamond St; admission free; ⏰visits by appointment, services 10am Sun; Ⓢ Susquehanna-Dauphin). A fine example of Gothic Revival architecture, this 1897 Episcopal church was a center of activism during the Civil Rights movement and the site of the National Conference of Black Power in 1968. However, it's for its series of protest art murals by Walter Edmonds and Richard Watson, created in the early 1970s, that the church is most notable. These amazing, occasionally violently in-your-face images place African American experiences and faces at the forefront.

## Honey's Sit 'n Eat
JEWISH $$

7 ⊗ MAP P104, E4

Jewish soul food such as latkes and French toast made with challah bread feature on the popular breakfast/brunch menu here. Feel virtuous ordering a vegan sloppy joe then sinful with a deep-fried cherry or apple pie. Expect to line up and it's cash only (but there's an ATM in the restaurant). (☎215-925-1150; http://honeyssitneat.com; 800 N 4th St, Northern Liberties; mains $9-15; ⏰7am-4pm Mon-Fri, to 5pm Sat & Sun; Ⓢ Spring Garden: Market-Frankford Line)

## Wm Mulherin's Sons
PIZZA $$

8 ⊗ MAP P104, G2

Gourmet pizzas – with toppings such as speck and eggs, and lamb and artichoke – take center stage at this appealing restaurant and bar in a creatively transformed old whiskey merchants building that is now a focus of Fishtown's hipster scene. Pasta and more substantial main dishes are also available, as well as a brunch menu on weekends. (☎267-753-9478; http://wmmulherinssons.com; 1355 N Front St, Fishtown; pizza $14-18, mains $29-31; ⏰5pm-midnight

Mon-Thu, to 1am Fri, 10:30am-2pm & 5pm-1am Sat & Sun; 🔊; S Girard: Market-Frankford Line)

## Joe's Steaks & Soda Shop

AMERICAN $

9 ⊗ MAP P104, G3

If you're hankering for a cheese-steak in Fishtown, Joe's is your an-swer. They come in small or large sizes and a variety of permutations including a vegan sandwich. The cozy booths, specialty sodas and great selection of complimentary sauces and pickles make it a prime place to tuck into Philly's signature sandwich. (📞215-423-5637; http://joessteaks.com; 1 W Girard Ave, Fishtown; cheesesteak from $6.75; 🕙11am-10pm Sun-Wed, to midnight Thu, to 3am Fri & Sat; S Girard: Market-Frankford Line)

## Kensington Quarters

AMERICAN $$

10 ⊗ MAP P104, G2

Nose to tail cooking is on offer at this buzzy restaurant and butchery. Sample its smokey Hungarian sausage with zingy pickles, bacon kielbasa with German potato salad, or go the full hog with the $100 mixed grill. The bar has eight taps and an interesting cocktail menu. (📞267-314-5086; www.kensingtonquarters.com; 1310 Frankford Ave, Fishtown; mains $11-30; 🕙5-10pm Mon-Thu, to 11pm Fri, 11:30am-2:30pm & 5-11pm Sat, 1:30am-2:30pm & 5-9pm Sun; S Girard: Market-Frankford Line)

## Silk City

DINER $$

11 ⊗ MAP P104, E5

This dining car and bar complex has been a fixture on Spring Garden St since the 1950s. It was revamped by new owners in 2007, with the dining car retaining its classic chrome-edged bar, button seat and booth layout. Brunch is served daily until 3:45pm and a dinner menu kicks in from 4pm to 1am. (📞215-592-8838; www.silkcityphilly.com; 435 Spring Garden St, Northern Liberties; mains $10-20; 🕙10am-2am; S Spring Garden: Market-Frankford Line)

## Suraya

LEBANESE $$

12 ⊗ MAP P104, G2

Like walking into a Lebanese bazaar, the front of this restaurant

## Pretzels & Bagels 🍽

Early-morning wanderers around Fishtown and Kens-ington can breakfast on warm pretzels straight from the oven at **Furfari's Soft Pretzels** (📞267-884-4204; 2025 Frankford Ave, Kensington; pretzel 40¢; 🕙1am-noon Mon-Sat; M Berks) or a freshly baked bagel from **Philly Style Bagels** (Map p104, H1; www.phillystylebagels.com; 1451 E Columbia Ave, Fishtown; bagels $2, sandwiches $9; 🕙7am-2pm Mon & Wed-Fri, 8am-2pm Sat & Sun; S Girard: Market-Frankford Line).

## Schmidt's Commons 👍

Built around a historic brewery **Schmidt's Commons** (Map p104, F3; https://theschmidtscommons.com; 1001 N 2nd St, Northern Liberties; S Girard: Market-Frankford Line) has a central 80,000-sq-ft piazza that hosts events such as craft markets, live music and salsa nights.

is stocked with an attractive selection of takeaway foods, homewares and cookbooks. It specializes in freshly baked *man'oushe* flatbread with a variety of toppings. Sample a selection of its other authentic dishes on the meze plate ($18). (☎ 215-302-1900; http://surayaphilly.com; 1528 Frankford Ave, Fishtown; ⊙ 7am-5pm Tue-Sun; S Girard: Market-Frankford Line)

## Cake Life Bake Shop    BAKERY $

**13** 🗺 MAP P104, G2

Who doesn't love a cupcake, especially when its cream icing is slathered in multicolored sprinkles? The winners of Food Network's Cupcake Wars have set up this cute bakery to share with the world their sweet and savory creations, which include gluten-free brownies, scones, sausage rolls and quiches. (☎ 215-278-2580; www.cakelifebakeshop.com; 1306 Frankford Ave, Fishtown; cupcakes $3;

⊙ 7am-7pm Tue-Thu, to 10pm Fri & Sat, 8am-4pm Sun; S Girard: Market-Frankford Line)

## Weckerly's Ice Cream    ICE CREAM $

**14** 🗺 MAP P104, G3

You'll find these delicious ice creams made with organic cream and free-range eggs in many places around town, but this is Weckerley's flagship store. Sample flavors such as Beard of Bees, made with local honey and crunchy almond clusters, or Jean Luc, an inspired combo of Earl Grey tea and marmalade. (☎ 215-423-2000; www.weckerlys.com; 9 W Girard Ave, Fishtown; ice-cream cup $4.75; ⊙ 3-10pm Mon-Thu, to 11pm Fri, noon-10pm Sat & Sun; S Girard: Market-Frankford Line)

# Drinking

## Trestle Inn    BAR

**15** 🍺 MAP P104, B6

On a dark corner this classed-up old dive is notable for its friendliness and craft cocktails, which can be enjoyed in a happy hour that lasts from 5pm until 8pm. From 9pm on Thursday and 10pm on Friday and Saturday go-go dancers get their groove on under the disco ball as DJs play hits from the 1960s onward. (☎ 267-239-0290; www.thetrestleinn.com; 339 N 11th St, Callowhill; ⊙ 5pm-1am Wed-Thu, to 2am Fri & Sat; S Spring Garden: Broad Street Line)

## The Random Tea Room

TEAHOUSE

16 📍 MAP P104, E5

This charming antique-style cafe dedicated to teas and infusions is practically unique in Philly. The 40-plus artisanal blends can be enjoyed by cup or pot, there's art on the walls by local artists and a tempting selection of bakes and savory nibbles, as well as chai oats. (📞267-639-2442; http://therandom tearoom.com; 713 N 4th St, Northern Liberties; ⏰10am-8pm; Ⓢ Spring Garden: Market-Frankford Line)

## La Colombe Fishtown

COFFEE

17 📍 MAP P104, G2

All the stops have been pulled out for the Philadelphia gourmet-coffee giant's flagship store in a converted Fishtown warehouse. Here you'll find a self-serve cafe, bakery and distillery producing Different Drum, a coffee-infused rum which you can sample in a variety of cocktails. The kitchen serves food until 3pm. (📞267-479-1600; www.lacolombe.com; 1335 Frankford Ave, Fishtown; ⏰7am-7pm Sun-Thu, to 9pm Fri & Sat; 🔊; Ⓢ Girard: Market-Frankford Line)

## W/N W/N Coffee Bar

COFFEE

18 📍 MAP P104, C5

Pronounced 'win win' this cafe-bar is run on a cooperative basis and has the feel of your coolest friend's living room. Apart from Elixir Coffee Roasters blends and a decent range of tea, there's a full bar and artisan pizza is served Wednesday to Saturday.

Weckerly's Ice Cream

# Craft Brewing Rennaisance

Prior to Prohibition these northeast areas of the city were awash with brewers and distillers. Today, history is repeating itself as microbreweries and craft distilleries are returning in force. Try the following:

**Philadelphia Distilling** (Map p104, G4; ☑ 215-671-0346; http://philadelphiadistilling.com; 25 E Allen St, Fishtown; tours $15; ☉ 4-11pm Thu & Fri, 1-11pm Sat & Sun; ⑤ Girard: Market-Frankford Line) The old Ajax Metal warehouse near the Delaware riverfront has been revamped into this impressive craft spirits operation, with a sophisticated bar and inventive cocktail list. One-hour informative tours start with a punch cocktail and finish with a tasting of the spirits range, including the award-winning Bluecoast American Dry.

**Yards Brewing Company** (Map p104, D5; ☑ 215-525-0175; www.yardsbrewing.com; 500 Spring Garden St, Spring Gardens; ☉ 11:30am-10pm Mon-Wed, to 11pm Thu & Fri, 11am-11pm Sat, to 10pm Sun; ⑤ Spring Garden: Market-Frankford Line) There are some 20 different beers on tap at this microbrewery that began life in 1994 and moved into this impressive new space in 2018. Sample a flight of four of its ales (some of which are named after the nation's Founding Fathers) for $7.

**New Liberty** (Map p104, F1; ☑ 1800-996-0595; https://newlibertydistillery.com; 1431 N Cadwallader St, Kensington; tours $15; ☉ 4-8pm Fri, noon-7pm, to 5pm; ⑤ Girard: Market-Frankford Line) Occupying the carriage house and old stables of an early-20th-century plumbing manufacturing company, New Liberty specializes in making rye whiskey, rum and vodka. In the tasting room you can sample all New Liberty's tipples straight or in cocktails. Tours, which include tastings, are held a couple of times a day on Saturday and Sunday, usually after 1pm.

**Evil Genius Beer Company** (Map p104, H1; ☑ 215-425-6820; http://evilgeniusbeer.com; 1727 N Front St, Fishtown; ☉ 4-10pm Wed & Thu, to midnight Fri, noon-midnight Sat, to 9pm Sun; ⑤ Berks) Silly names – Purple Monkey Dishwater (a chocolate peanut porter) and Ma! The Meatloaf (a Belgium white ale) – for serious beer is this brewery's stock in trade. Sample a flight of five for $12 with 5oz tasters going for $2.50.

**Urban Village** (Map p104, F3; ☑ 267-687-1961; http://urbanvillagebrewing.com/; 1001 N 2nd St, Northern Liberties; ☉ 11am-midnight; ⑤ Girard: Market-Frankford Line) The ales brewed and served at this spacious microbrewery change weekly, but you can expect plenty of IPAs as well as more adventurous styles such as a fruity sour gose or a kolish hybrid. It's also known for oven-fired pizzas.

A fun lineup of regular events, including live jazz and queer and feminist karaoke, add to the appeal. (www.winwincoffeebar.com; 931 Spring Garden St, Poplar; ⏱4pm-midnight Wed, Thu & Sun, to 2am Fri & Sat; Ⓢ Spring Garden: Broad Street Line)

### One Shot Cafe

COFFEE

19 Ⓜ MAP P104, F3

This attractive cafe offers an elegant old-world space downstairs with circular marble-topped tables and a pressed-tin ceiling, while upstairs is a wonderfully cozy library lounge with squishy leather sofas. It serves Stumptown coffee and has a decent food menu. (📞215-627-1620; www.1shotcoffee.com; 217 W George St, Northern Liberties; ⏱7am-5pm; Ⓢ Girard: Market-Frankford Line)

### El Bar

BAR

20 Ⓜ MAP P104, G2

Dimly lit, cash-only dive bar that takes its name from the elevated tracks of the Market-Frankford Line right outside. There's a pool table as well as a beer garden decorated with junk. (📞215-634-6430; 1356 N Front St, Fishtown; ⏱11am-2am; Ⓢ Girard: Market-Frankford Line)

### Frankford Hall

BEER GARDEN

21 Ⓜ MAP P104, G3

With an open courtyard and interior space set up like a classic German beer garden, Frankford Hall offers long shared tables and a bar serving a generous menu of German, American and specialty ales alongside pretzels, sausages and burgers. (📞215-634-3338; www.frankfordhall.com; 1210 Frankford Ave, Fishtown; ⏱4pm-2am Mon-Fri, noon-2am Sat, 11:30am-2am Sun; Ⓢ Girard: Market-Frankford Line)

### Goose Island Brewhouse

CRAFT BEER

22 Ⓜ MAP P104, G4

Chicago's Goose Island craft brewery's spiffy new operation is in an old dry ice factory near the river. There's a great range of beers on tap including IPAs, stouts and ciders, and a good food menu. Outdoor seating, too. (📞215-560-8181; www.gooseisland.com; 1002 Canal St, Fishtown; ⏱4-11pm Mon-Thu, to midnight Fri, 11am-midnight Sat, to 11pm Sun; Ⓢ Girard: Market-Frankford Line)

## Entertainment

### PhilaMOCA

PERFORMING ARTS

23 ✪ MAP P104, B5

A former tombstone store, then producer Diplo's studios, this eclectic space now has an equally eclectic program of cult movie nights, live-music shows, art, comedy and more. (Philadelphia Mausoleum of Contemporary Art; 📞267-519-9651; www.philamoca.org; 531 N 12th St, Poplar; Ⓢ Spring Garden: Broad Street Line)

## Pig Iron Theatre Company

THEATER

24 ⭐ MAP P104, F2

One of Philly's most exciting and original contemporary theater companies, Pig Iron shows can be bizarre combinations of vaudeville, clowning and silence, by turns hilarious and surreal. This is the company's studio space, which very occasionally is open for performances. (📞215-425-1100; www.pigiron.org; 1417 N 2nd St, Fishtown; ⑤Girard: Market-Frankford Line)

## Johnny Brenda's

LIVE MUSIC

25 ⭐ MAP P104, G3

One of the hubs of Philly's indie-rock scene, this is a great small venue with a balcony, plus a solid restaurant and bar with equally indie-minded beers. (📞215-739-9684; www.johnnybrendas.com; 1201 N Frankford Ave, Fishtown; tickets $10-15; 🕑kitchen 11am-1am, showtimes vary; ⑤Girard: Market-Frankford Line)

## Union Transfer

CONCERT VENUE

26 ⭐ MAP P104, B5

Opened in 2011, this music hall is one of the best spaces in Philly for bigger-name bands, with eclectic shows and good bar service. (📞215-232-2100; www.utphilly.com; 1026 Spring Garden St, Poplar; tickets $15-40; ⑤Spring Garden: Broad Street Line)

## The Fillmore

LIVE MUSIC

27 ⭐ MAP P104, G4

With room for up to 2500 spectators, this is one of Philly's largest live-music venues. Upstairs is the more intimate 450-person Foundry space, which is used for newer acts and DJ dance parties. (📞215-309-0150; www.thefillmore philly.com; 29 E Allen St, Fishtown; ⑤Girard: Market-Frankford Line)

## Punch Line Philly

COMEDY

28 ⭐ MAP P104, G4

This 300-seat comedy club, restaurant and bar is part of a small national chain of similar comedy venues. The lineup includes established acts as well as up-and-coming performers. Every Saturday at 11am they host a drag diva brunch. (📞215-606-6555; www.punchlinephilly.com; 33 E Laurel St, Fishtown; tickets $18.50-30.00; ⑤Girard: Market-Frankford Line)

# Shopping

## Amalgum Comics & Coffeehouse

BOOKS

29 🅰 MAP P104, H1

Reveling in geek culture is this mashup of a comic book store and cafe, the passion project of owner Ariell Johnson. Check its Facebook page for details of the many events held here including anime screenings, monthly book clubs and author signings. (☎215-427-3300; www.amalgamphilly.com; 2578 Frankford Ave, Kensington; ⊙7am-8pm Tue-Fri, 8am-8pm Sat, 10am-6pm Sun; Ⓢ Huntingdon)

## Casa Papel
STATIONERY

**30** 🔒 MAP P104, F5

Apart from being a treasure trove of sheets in a variety of shades, textures and patterns, this colorful store also offers custom graphic design and specialty printing. (☎267-761-9149; www.casapapel.com; 804 N 2nd St, Northern Liberties; Ⓢ Spring Garden: Market-Frankford Line)

## Architectural Antiques Exchange
ANTIQUES

**31** 🔒 MAP P104, F5

No one will have room in their suitcases for the architectural artifacts and one-off antique furnishings on sale here, but it's still fun to poke around its two floors of wares to see what's on offer. (☎215-922-3669; http://architecturalantiques.com; 709-715 N 2nd St, Northern Liberties; ⊙10am-5pm Mon-Sat; Ⓢ Spring Garden: Market-Frankford Line)

## Art Star
ARTS & CRAFTS

**32** 🔒 MAP P104, F5

Lovers of knickknacks and cute gifts will be in heaven at this showcase for US-based creatives. Art Star stocks a wide range of arts, crafts, stationery and fashion items. Exhibitions and craft workshops are held here, too (☎215-238-1557; www.artstarphilly.com; 623 N 2nd St, Northern Liberties; ⊙11am-7pm Tue-Sat, noon-6pm Sun; Ⓢ Spring Garden: Market-Frankford Line)

## R E Load
FASHION & ACCESSORIES

**33** 🔒 MAP P104, F5

What to do when you're not happy with the messenger bags available? Design your own was the solution of R E Load's founders Ronnie and Ellie. Check out the range of the brand's custom-made premium bags here, as well as other items such as caps and wallets. (☎215-625-2987; www.reloadbags.com; 608 N 2nd St, Northern Liberties; Ⓢ Spring Garden: Market-Frankford Line)

## Norman Porter
FASHION & ACCESSORIES

**34** 🔒 MAP P104, G1

Designers and makers Michael and David Stampler named their high-quality selvedge denim jeans after their grandfather. These cult fashion threads are not cheap (around $250 a pair) but are extremely well-made and guaranteed to last a generation. (☎267-908-4694; www.normanporter.com; 150 Cecil B Moore Ave, Kensington; ⊙10am-6pm Fri by appointment; Ⓢ Berks)

# Walking Tour 🚶

# Germantown Amble

*The location of Philadelphia's only revolutionary battlefield, Germantown was once a remote summertime retreat for the city's rich and powerful. It later became an important stop on the Underground Railroad. Today it's a fascinating community where grand old mansions sit cheek by jowl with beauty salons and pawn shops.*

## Getting There

🚇 Germantown station is close to Germantown Ave.

🚌 23 will also take you to Germantown

### ❶ Historic Germantown

Pick up leaflets and an area map at this **visitor center** (☏215-844-1683; www.freedomsbackyard.com; 5501 Germantown Ave; museum adult/student/child $3/2/free; ⏲9am-1pm Tue, 9am-5pm Thu, 1st & 3rd Sun by appointment), library and small museum showcasing 18th-century interiors.

### ❷ Grumblethorpe

Built in 1744 it was in **Grumblethorpe** (☏215-843-4820; www.philalandmarks.org/grumblethorpe; 5267 Germantown Ave; adult/student/child $8/6/free; ⏲noon-4pm 2nd Sat of month Apr-Oct, by appointment 10am-3pm Tue-Thu) that British Brigadier-General James Agnew died during the Revolutionary War – his blood stains can still be seen on the floor!

### ❸ Uncle Bobbie's Coffee & Books

This excellent **bookstore and cafe** (☏215-403-7058; www.unclebobbies.com; 5445 Germantown Ave; ⏲7am-9pm Mon-Thu, to 11pm Fri, 8am-11pm Sat, 8am-7pm Sun; 🛜) has a laser focus on black writers and literature. Browse the wonderful range of tomes and own-brand goods including t-shirts and totes.

### ❹ Wyck

Famed for its lovely garden planted with 50-plus cultivars of heritage roses, **Wyck** (☏215-848-1690; http://wyck.org; 6026 Germantown Ave; garden free, house suggested donation $8; ⏲noon-4pm Thu-Sat Apr-Nov) was renovated by William Strickland in 1824 and is furnished with many original family belongings.

### ❺ Ebenezer Maxwell Mansion

This striking Victorian Gothic **mansion** (☏215-438-1861; http://ebenezermaxwellmansion.org; 200 W Tulpehocken St; tour $7; ⏲hourly tours from 12.15-3.15pm Thu-Sat) has been meticulously restored and decorated with Renaissance and Rococo revival furniture.

### ❻ Johnson House

This modest stone **house** (☏215-438-1768; www.johnsonhouse.org; 6306 Germantown Ave; adult/student/child $8/6/4; ⏲tours 1:15, 2:15 & 3:15pm Thu & Fri Feb-Jun & Sep-Nov; 🚃23, 🚇Upsal) built by an abolitionist Quaker family became a station on the Underground Railroad in 1858.

### ❼ Cliveden

The bloody Battle of Germantown was fought **here** (☏215-848-1777; www.cliveden.org; 6401 Germantown Ave; tours adult/student/child $10/8/free; ⏲grounds open daily, house noon-4pm Thu-Sun Apr-Dec; 🚃23, 🚇Upsal) in 1777. During the Revolutionary Germantown Festival in October the British defeat of the Patriots is reenacted.

# Explore ⓢ
# South Philadelphia

Sprawling South Philadelphia will appeal to those in search of multicultural diversity as encapsulated in the historic South 9th Street Italian Market. Hard-scrabble in some parts, gentrifying in others, this Philly district covers Queen Village, home to Fabric Row; the hip gourmet strip of East Passyunk Ave, the repurposed Navy Yards, FDR Park and the city's major sports stadiums.

The area's two main sights – South 9th Street Italian Market (p120) and Philadelphia's Magic Gardens (p124) – are close to each other, and both can easily be seen in half a day. Other sights are widely scattered with the Mummers Museum (p124) and Gloria Dei Church (p124) close to each other on the area's east side, and FDR Park (p125), the American Swedish Historical Museum (p125) and the Navy Yard (p128) all a long way south at the end of Broad St.

## Getting There & Around

🚌 SEPTA buses follow straight north–south routes through this district.

Ⓢ Also useful for accessing the area is the Broad Street Line subway, which stops between Lombard-South and AT&T (the end of the line).

## Neighborhood Map on p122

South St, Philadelphia JAMES KIRKIKIS/SHUTTERSTOCK ©

Top Sight 📷

# South 9th Street Italian Market

*This long and vibrant commercial strip is lined with fresh produce stalls that sell their wares under awnings on the street. Stores include traditional butchers, fishmongers and delis. The northern end is still predominantly Italian; south of Washington St skews Mexican, so you can pick up tortillas and tortellini in the same trip.*

◎ MAP P122, E2

📞 215-278-2903

http://italianmarket philly.org

9th St btwn Fitzwater & Wharton Sts, Bella Vista

🕗 8am-5pm Tue-Sat, to 3pm Sun

🚌 47, Ⓢ Ellsworth-Federal

## Speciality Stores

Mondays are traditionally a day off for some vendors, but the market is still open as are several of the shops, the pick of which are:

**Di Bruno Bros** (📞 215-922.-2876; https://dibruno.com; 930 S 9th St; ⏰ 9am-5pm Mon, to 6pm Tue-Thu, 8am-6pm Fri & Sat, 8am-4pm Sun) Deli (pictured left) specialising in cheese, olives and charcuterie.

**Cappuccio's Meats** (📞 215-922-5792; 1019 S 9th St; ⏰ 8am-5pm Mon-Wed, to 6pm Thu & Fri, 7am-6pm Sat, 8am-3pm Sun) Butchers famed for its spirals of *chevalata* (a pork sausage made with provolone cheese and parsley).

**Grassia's** (📞 215-627-8039; www.italianmarketspiceco.com; 949 S 9th St; ⏰ 8am-5pm Tue-Sat, 9am-2pm Sun) Sells spices and hot sauces.

**Cardenas** (📞 267-928-3690; https://cardenastaproom.com; 942 S 9th St; ⏰ 10am-5:30pm Mon-Fri, 9am-5pm Sat, 10am-3pm Sun) Taste a vast range of olive oils and balsamic vinegar.

**Fante's Kitchen Shop** (📞 215-922-5557; www.fantes.com; 1006 S 9th St; ⏰ 9am-5pm Tue-Sat, 9:30am-1:30pm Sun) Packed with all the kitchen gadgets of your dreams.

## Rocky & Rizzo

The market gained wider fame for Rocky Balboa's famous training run along 9th St in the 1976 Oscar-winner *Rocky*. A mural of ex-mayor **Frank Rizzo** (cnr 9th & Montrose Sts) is a prominent landmark. It's one of the most vandalized murals in the city, a reflection of Rizzo's controversial status.

---

### ★ Top Tips

○ Stop by the Visitor Center to pick up a map and discount coupons before you go shopping.

○ **Taste4Travel** (📞 610-506-6120; www.taste4travel.net; Italian Market tour $60) market tours are led by Jacqueline Peccina-Kelly, a professional chef who grew up in the area and knows many of the shop owners.

---

### ✗ Take a Break

**Anthony's** (📞 215-627-2586; www.italiancoffeehouse.com; 905 S 9th St; ⏰ 7am-7pm, to 8:30pm Sat, to 5:30pm Sun; 📶) is the classic Italian Market spot for espresso, cannoli and panini.

**Center City Pretzel Co** (📞 215-463-5664; www.centercitypretzel.com; 816 Washington Ave, Passyunk Sq; pretzel 40¢; ⏰ 4am-noon Mon-Sat, 6:30-10.30am Sun; 🚌 47, Ⓢ Ellsworth-Federal) Fresh classic pretzels warm from the oven.

South Philadelphia

**For reviews see**

| | | |
|---|---|---|
| ⊙ | Top Sights | p120 |
| ⊙ | Sights | p124 |
| ⊗ | Eating | p126 |
| ⊙ | Drinking | p130 |
| ✪ | Entertainment | p131 |
| 🔒 | Shopping | p134 |

Lombard-South St

WASHINGTON SQUARE WEST

Seger Park

⊙7 Atlas of Tomorrow
South St

Bainbridge St

⊙1 Philadelphia's Magic Gardens

Fitzwater St

HAWTHORNE

Catharine St
Webster St
Christian St
Montrose St
Hall St

Carpenter St
Kimball St

S 11th St
S 10th St

24

S 18th St
S 17th St
S 16th St
S 15th St

Broad St

Washington Ave

Ellsworth-Federal Ⓜ

Ellsworth St

⊗29 Alter St

Federal St

S 13th St
S 12th St

Annin St

Wharton St

Titan St

Geno's Steaks

Capitolo Playground

Columbus Square

Reed St

Pat's King of Steaks 🔒21

Electric Street

Reed St

Dickinson St

Gerritt St
Wilder St

SOUTH PHILADELPHIA

Wilder St
Dickinson St
Greenwich St
Cross St

🔒33

S Juniper St
S Clarion St
S 13th St

Tasker St

Linn St

⊗19
⊗9
⊗14

Morris St

Fernon St
Mountain St

S 10th St
S 9th St

Morris St

S 17th St
S 16th St
S 15th St

⊗8

S Watts St
S 13th St
Camac St
Iseminger St

Castle Ave

Moore St

E Passyunk Ave

17

⊗11

Mifflin St

McKean St

⊗10

Bok Bar

A B C D

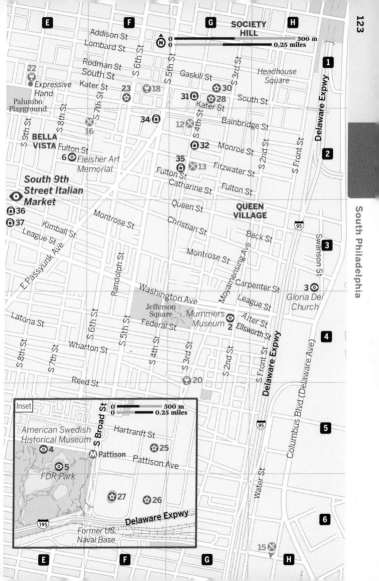

South Philadelphia

**SOCIETY HILL**

0 — 500 m
0 — 0.25 miles

Addison St
Lombard St
Rodman St
South St
Kater St
Gaskill St
Headhouse Square
South St
Kater St
Bainbridge St
Monroe St
Fitzwater St
Catharine St
Fulton St
Queen St
Christian St
Beck St
Montrose St
Carpenter St
League St
Washington Ave
Mummers Museum
Alter St
Ellsworth St
Federal St
Wharton St
Reed St

22
Expressive Hand
Palumbo Playground
23
18
31
30
28
34
12
32
35
13
36
37

**BELLA VISTA**
Fleisher Art Memorial
6

**South 9th Street Italian Market**

**QUEEN VILLAGE**

Gloria Dei Church
3

Jefferson Square
2
20

S 9th St
S 8th St
S 7th St
S 6th St
S 5th St
S 4th St
S 3rd St
S 2nd St
S Front St
Swanson St
Delaware Expwy
Columbus Blvd (Delaware Ave)

E Passyunk Ave
Kimball St
League St
Latona St
Montrose St
Randolph St

Fulton St

Delaware Expwy

Inset
0 — 500 m
0 — 0.25 miles

American Swedish Historical Museum
4
FDR Park
5

Hartranft St
Pattison
25
Pattison Ave
27
26
Delaware Expwy
Former US Naval Base

S Broad St

15

# Sights

## Philadelphia's Magic Gardens

GARDENS

**1**  MAP P122, D1

The ongoing life's work of mosaic mural artist Isaiah Zagar, this is a folk-art wonderland of mirror mosaics, bottle walls and quirky sculpture. Zagar's mosaic murals can be seen around the city – visit here first, and you'll know what to look for. It also hosts small exhibitions of other artists' work with a focus on those who are self-taught and making mosaics or folk-art works.

Between November and March site tours (adult/student/child $15/12/8) are held at 3pm on Saturday and Sunday. Between April and October there walking tours around the area at 3pm Friday through Sunday. (☏215-733-0390; www.phillymagicgardens.org; 1020 South St, Bella Vista; adult/student/child $10/8/5; ⏰11am-6pm Wed-Mon, to 8pm Fri & Sat Apr-Oct; 🚌23, 40)

## Mummers Museum

MUSEUM

**2**  MAP P122, G4

Learn to tell your Fancy Brigades from your String Bands at this fun museum devoted to the unique tradition of Philadelphia Mummery. Reflecting the many immigrant cultures and traditions of settlers in the city, Mummers divisions famously parade on New Year's Day down Broad St. Here you can see many of the fabulous costumes worn over the years and even try some on.

On Thursday evenings from May through September the museum holds a free outdoor string band concert and block party starting at 8pm, where you may be able to learn the Mummers Strut dance steps. (☏215-336-3050; www.mummersmuseum.com; 1100 S 2nd St, Pennsport; admission by donation; ⏰9:30am-4pm Wed-Sat; 🚌4, 57)

## Gloria Dei Church

CHURCH

**3**  MAP P122, H3

Philadelphia's original settlers were Swedish Lutherans and this is the site of one of their first churches, built between 1698 and 1700. It's made of brick and was designed by English carpenters and masons. The simple, elegant interior of the chapel is notable for the models of the ships *Fogel*

---

### Electric Street

Best visited at twilight when its neon colors have an inky blue sky backdrop, the art installation **Electric Street** (Map p122, D4; Percy St, Passyunk Sq; 🚌45, 47, Ⓢ Ellsworth-Federal) is a collaborative work by mural artist David Guinn and light artist Drew Billiau with the financial help of Mural Arts and the Knight Foundation. It has transformed what was a crime-ridden alley where people illegally dumped trash into a thing of beauty.

*Grip* and *Kalmar Nyckel*, which hang from the ceiling. These are the vessels that brought a group of Swedes to the area in 1643. (Old Swedes Church; 📞215-389-1513; www.old-swedes.org; 916 S Swanson St, Pennsport; ⊙9am-4pm Tue-Sun; 🚃25, 57)

## American Swedish Historical Museum

MUSEUM

4 ⊙ MAP P122, E5

The oldest Swedish-American museum in the US was founded in 1926. Its handsome building, designed by Swedish-American architect John Nydén, is partly modeled after a 17th-century Swedish manor house, and contains 12 gorgeous exhibition galleries with a fascinating set of items. A highlight is the painted ceiling and wall murals in the Grand Hall by Christian von Schneidau. (📞215-389-1776; www.americanswedish.org; 1900 Pattison Ave, South Philadelphia; adult/student/child $10/7/5; ⊙10am-4pm Tue-Fri, noon-4pm Sat & Sun; 🚇AT&T)

## FDR Park

PARK

5 ⊙ MAP P122, E5

The attractive 340-acre FDR Park includes fields and lakes, making it the perfect spot to relax in greenery-starved South Philadelphia. Locals love to picnic here in the summer and also use the park's facilities for boating, tennis, golf and other sports. (www.fdrpark.org; 1500 Pattison Ave, South Philadelphia; ⊙6am-9pm; 🚇AT&T)

Mummers Museum

JAMES KIRKIKIS/SHUTTERSTOCK ©

## Fleisher Art Memorial

ARTS CENTER

6 ⊙ MAP P122, E2

A wide variety of classes and workshops are held at this art school, founded in 1898. Parts of the building are worth a look as it includes the Romanesque Revival Episcopal Church of the Evangelist, designed by Frank Furness. The sanctuary includes stained-glass windows by John La Farge, a mural by Robert Henri and an altarpiece on the life of Moses by Violet Oakley.

Samuel Fleisher, the heir to a successful late-19th-century woolen mill, founded the college as a means for the children of his factory workers to enjoy free art classes. That principle of making art accessible to all, regardless of economic means, continues today. Classes book out as soon as registration starts. While here also look for the beautiful mural **Autumn Revisited** (www.muralarts. org/artworks/autumn-revisited). (☑215-922-3456; www.fleisher.org; 719 Catharine St, Bella Vista; ☺9am-9:30pm Mon-Thu, to 4pm Fri & Sat; 🚌40, 47)

## Atlas of Tomorrow

PUBLIC ART

7 ⊙ MAP P122, C1

The subtitle of Candy Chang's interactive mural is 'a device for philosophical reflection' and it embodies the idea of art as meditation and a tool for mental health. Beneath a monochrome image made up of over 200,000 dots that were finger painted by Chang and the local community is a giant dial. Spin this to land on one of 64 fables inspired by the *I Ching* that you can read for poetic guidance. (www. muralarts.org/artworks/the-atlas-of -tomorrow/; 533 S Juniper St, Center City; 🚌40, 23, Ⓢ Lombard-South St)

# Eating

## Hardena/Waroeng Surabaya

INDONESIAN $

8 ✂ MAP P122, A5

Short of a trip to Jakarta you are unlikely to find better authentic Indonesian food than that served at James Beard–nominated Hardena. Order at the counter the superb-value rice plates with a choice of two dishes, or go the whole hog with a *rijsttafel* platter ($25) that includes eight dishes plus crackers and satay. (☑215-271-9442; www.face book.com/pg/hardena.waroengsura baya; 1754 S Hicks St, Newbold; mains from $8; ☺11:30am-8:30pm Wed-Mon; Ⓢ Tasker-Morris)

## Noord

EUROPEAN $$

9 ✂ MAP P122, C5

Think Dutch comfort food rather than new-Scandi cuisine at this welcoming BYOB just off the main E Passyunk drag. Jovial Netherlands-born chef Joncarl Lachman offers dishes such as *gehaktballen* (sirloin meatballs) and herring sliders, and makes a very generous and delicious seafood stew.

There are many tempting and out-of-the-ordinary options on the

## Mummers Parade

Said to be the oldest continual folk festival in the US, the origins of Philadelphia's **Mummers Parade** (http://phillymummers.com; ⏱ Jan 1) are contested. Some say its roots go back to a Swedish and Finnish custom of going around to visit neighbors between Christmas and New Year, others believe it is based on the English Mummery Play, a kind of burlesque with harlequins dressed in shiny costumes. In German, *mummerkleid* means 'fancy dress' and mummenspiel means masquerade, so maybe that's where the idea came from. Regardless, it's believed the first Mummers brigades appeared in the 1700s parading in the Washington Ave area. In 1901, an official site – on Broad St from South Philadelphia to City Hall – was ordained for the New Year's Day parade.

As with Mardi Gras, it's the costumes in a rainbow of shades with industrial quantities of sequins, sparkles and plumage that are the highlight of the parade. Each year features a different theme, necessitating brand-new costumes for which little expense is spared. Despite its longevity and popularity, the Mummers are not without controversy. Relatively few women and hardly any people of color are in the troupes. Some troupes also paint their faces, mimicking racial stereotypes.

The parade starts at 7am and can go on as long as 12 hours. If you're not in town for the New Year's Day parade you may be able to catch Mummers bands playing at the **Mummers Museum** (p124) and at other special events such as Manayunk's Mardi Gras (www.mummersmardigras.com) at the end of February.

Sunday brunch menu, too, such as vinegar-braised beef with Gouda. (☎ 267-909-9704; www.noordphilly.com; 1046 Tasker St, East Passyunk; mains $19-28; ⏱ 5-10pm Wed & Thu, to 10:30pm Fri & Sat, 11am-2pm & 5-9pm Sun; 🚌 45, 47, Ⓢ Tasker-Morris)

### Le Virtù ITALIAN $$$

10 ❌ MAP P122, B6

Chef Joe Cicala is dedicated, obsessively so, to the cuisine of Abruzzo, the region east of Rome, where he long studied with home cooks. Old-school ways are married wherever possible with the cream of local produce. Tuesdays are BYOB. (☎ 215-271-5626; http://levirtu.com; 1927 E Passyunk Ave, East Passyunk; mains $23-36, degustation menu from $45; ⏱ 5-10pm Mon-Thu, to 10:30pm Fri & Sat, 4-9:30pm Sun; Ⓢ Snyder)

## Navy Yard

A short walk south of FDR Park brings you to the gates of the **Navy Yard** (www.navyyard.org; 4747 S Broad St, South Philadelphia; **S** AT&T). Philadelphia was the birthplace of the US Navy and ships were built and repaired in this yard up until 1996. The Navy still uses the site to store decommissioned vessels, but for several years now the yard has successfully functioned as a business campus for companies such as GlaxoSmithKline and Urban Outfitters, whose headquarters stand in the shadow of the mammoth aircraft carrier *John F Kennedy*. Look out for **Central Green**, an attractive 4.5-acre park designed by landscape architect James Corner (of New York City High Line fame), with a running track, ping-pong tables, hammocks and yellow painted Adirondack chairs. Beside the park is **1200 Intrepid**, a striking piece of contemporary architecture by Bjarke Ingels – the office building's angled concrete facade recalls both a giant wave and the bow of a ship.

### Saté Kampar
MALAYSIAN $

11 ✖ MAP P122, B6

You will not find more authentic or delicious Malaysian food in Philadelphia than that served here. Skewers of meat or tofu are grilled to order and come with a classic Malay peanut sauce or a Hainanese sauce sweetened with pineapple. (☏267-324-3860; www.facebook.com/satekampar; 1837 E Passyunk Ave, East Passyunk; mains $12-15; ⏰11:30am-2:30pm & 5-10pm; **S** Snyder)

### Famous 4th Street Delicatessen
DELI $$

12 ✖ MAP P122, G2

In business since 1923, this corner Jewish deli is famous for its mon-ster-sized sandwiches, big enough for two to share. The menu is a roll-call of Jewish soul food, from chopped liver to hot corned beef and even matzoh brei (an omelet made with matzoh). (☏215-922-3274; www.famous4thstreetdelicatessen.com; 700 S 4th St, Queen Village; sandwiches $18-24; ⏰8am-9pm; 🚌40, 57)

### Hungry Pigeon
AMERICAN $$

13 ✖ MAP P122, G2

Although it's a pleasant spot for breakfast or a drink at its bar, Hungry Pigeon comes into its own for dinner, when chefs Scott Schroeder and Pat O'Malley flex their culinary talents. You can let them choose what to serve or pick from dishes that may include roasted beet salad, pasta fagioli or a pot roast. (☏215-278-2736; www.hungrypigeon.com; 743 S 4th St, Queen Village; mains $16-28, 4-course dinner $45; ⏰7am-11pm Mon-Thu, to midnight Fri, 9am-midnight Sat & Sun; 🚌40, 57)

## Townsend

FRENCH $$$

14 MAP P122, C5

Townsend Wentz's elegant, white-tablecloth restaurant is a dream date spot. Service is excellent and the food is delicious if sometimes a little skimpy on the portions. If you're hankering for dishes such as a melt-in-the-mouth seared foie gras or a perfectly roasted barramundi then you won't be disappointed. ( 267-639-3203; www.townsendrestaurant.com; 1623 E Passyunk Ave, East Passyunk; mains $28-34; 5pm-2am Wed-Sun; 47, S Tasker-Morris)

## John's Roast Pork

SANDWICHES $

15 MAP P122, H6

True Philly cheesesteak (er, porksteak...cheesepork?!) served with true Philly atmosphere: no frills, better-have-your-cash-ready-or-else, yelling when needed, and cash only. But the line goes out the door for good reason: these are as good as a Philly-style sandwich gets. It's well worth the detour to this family-run joint that's been around since 1930. ( 215-463-1951; www.johnsroastpork.com; 14 E Snyder Ave, Pennsport; sandwiches $6-12; 9am-7pm Tue-Sat; 25, 79)

## Fitzwater Cafe

DINER $

16 MAP P122, F2

A South Philly classic diner, no-nonsense waitresses serve generous all-day breakfast dishes at this handsome cash-only joint in a former gas station. If you're going for pancakes, trust us: a short stack will be plenty. ( 215-629-

Geno's Steaks (p130)

## Cheesesteaks Stand-off

Take the taste test between the originator **Pat's King of Steaks** (Map p122, D4; ☎215-468-1546; www.patskingofsteaks.com; 1237 E Passyunk Ave, Passyunk Sq; cheesesteak $11; ☺24hr; ☒45, 47, ⑤Ellsworth-Central) and the neon-bedecked upstart **Geno's Steaks** (Map p122, D4; ☎215-389-0659; www.genosteaks.com; 1219 S 9th St; cheesesteak from $10; ☺24hr), who square off against each other across E Passyunk Ave.

Order 'wit' (with) or 'widdout' (without) onions, and with your choice of cheese (Whiz, American or provolone). Cash only and have the money ready because the line moves fast.

0428; 728 S 7th St, Bella Vista; mains $8-15; ☺7am-3am; ☒47)

# Drinking

## Second District Brewing

MICROBREWERY

17 🅟 MAP P122, A6

A converted auto workshop is the location for this South Philly microbrewery that's one to watch. They like to experiment with their brewing here, so there's bound to be something interesting and unique on the menu of 10 draft beers, such as the Entwife, an English-style dark mild beer, or the cave-aged (and potent) barleywine. (☎215-575-5900; http://seconddistrictbrewing.com; 1939 S Bancroft St, Newbold; ☺11am-midnight; ☒2, ⑤Snyder)

## Tattooed Mom

BAR

18 🅟 MAP P122, F1

It feels a little disrespectful to call such a fun and fabulously deco-rated place a 'dive bar', but the friendly staff and patrons of Tattooed Mom likely wouldn't mind and that label just easily sums up the bar's casual, welcome-to-all nature. (☎215-238-9880; www.tattooedmomphilly.com; 530 South St, Queen Village; ☺noon-2am; ☒40, 47)

## Manatawny Still Works

COCKTAIL BAR

19 🅟 MAP P122, C5

This Pottstown distillery's craft spirits are served in this tasting room. Sample them in a flight ($15) or go for a creative cocktail such as Art & Stormy, which pairs its barrel-aged rum with rhubarb bitters, or the vodka-based Italian Market, which comes with a side of tasty blue cheese. (☎267-679-0537; www.manatawnystillworks.com; 1603 E Passyunk Ave, East Passyunk; ☺5-11pm Mon-Thu, noon-11pm Fri & Sat, to 8pm Sun; ☒45, 47, ⑤Tasker-Morris)

## Herman's Coffee
COFFEE

20 MAP P122, G4

This chilled cafe is based in an old auto repair shop and named after the owner's granddad. Beans are roasted on-site for its pour-over brews, while fancy teas are also on offer. Every Sunday a different food truck pulls up outside to serve brunch. (www.hermanscoffee. com; 1313 S 3rd St, Pennsport; 6am-6pm Mon-Fri, from 7am Sat & Sun; 57)

## Garage Passyunk
CRAFT BEER

21 MAP P122, D4

There's no excuse for not finding a beer you like at this place: their coolers are stocked with over 400 different cans, including many limited-edition ales. You can BYO food from the local cheesesteak stalls or check out the options from the on-premises food truck. Another plus: games such as pool and shuffleboard. (215-278-2429; www.garagephilly.com; 1231 E Passyunk Ave, Passyunk Sq; 5pm-2am Mon-Fri, 11am-2am Sat & Sun; 47)

## Chapterhouse Cafe & Gallery
CAFE

22 MAP P122, E1

Coffees and teas made with organic and fair-trade beans and leaves are served in this arty cafe that has frequently changing shows featuring local creatives. (215-238-2626; https://chapterhousecafe. wordpress.com; 620 S 9th St, Bella Vista; 7am-10pm; 40, 47)

# Entertainment

## L'etage
CABARET

23 MAP P122, F1

Great cabaret, club nights and other events all happen here. Shows could be a tryout of a new musical, male queer 'boylesque', or, on rare occasions, Martha Graham Cracker, alter ego of Dito Van Reigersberg and one of Philly's top drag talents.

The downstairs crêperie (noon to 9pm Tuesday to Thursday, until 10pm Friday, 10am to 10pm Saturday, 10am to 9pm Sunday) serves authentic savory and sweet crêpes in a cozy space with a fireplace.

### Expressive Hand

If you've been inspired by the mosaic murals around South Philly, you can create your own mini-version at **Expressive Hand** (Map p122, E1; 267-519-2626; www.expressivehand.com; 622 S 9th St, Bella Vista; from $5; noon-8pm Wed, 10:30am-9pm Thu-Sat, noon-6pm Sun; Lombard-South Station), as well as paint your own design on a range of ready-fired ceramic pieces. Prices are all-inclusive and walk-ins are welcome. To aid creativity, BYOB is also possible.

### Bok Bar

Take in a panoramic view of the city from the seasonal **Bok Bar** (Map p122, D6; ☎215-220-6815; www.bok-bar.com; 800 Mifflin St, East Passyunk; ⏰5-11pm Wed, to midnight Fri, to 1am Sat, noon-10pm Sun, end May-end Sep; 🚌45, 47, Ⓢ Tasker-Morris), located on the roof of a creative community of work spaces and artist studios that have colonized the one-time Bok Technical High School. Check the website for special events, including dance parties and pop-up dinners.

(☎215-592-0656; http://creperie -beaumonde.com; 624 S 6th St, Queen Village; ⏰7:30pm-1am Tue-Thu & Sun, 7pm-2am Fri & Sat; 🚌40, 47)

### Philadelphia Clef Club of Jazz and Performing Arts

LIVE MUSIC

24 ⭐ MAP P122, C1

This jazz institution evolved from the Local 274, a black musician's union formed in 1935 when racism and segregation prohibited African Americans from joining the city's other musician unions. The membership log includes greats such as John Coltrane, Dizzy Gillespie and Grover Washington Jr. Check online for details of monthly performances (some free) and film screenings. (☎215-893-9912; http:// clefclubofjazz.org; 738 S Broad St, Graduate Hospital; Ⓢ Lombard-South)

### Citizens Bank Park

SPECTATOR SPORT

25 ⭐ MAP P122, F5

Home to Philadelphia Phillies baseball team, this 43,000-seat ball park boasts great sight lines and close proximity to the field, as well as panoramic views toward distant downtown Philly.

Tours (adult/child $10/6) of the ball park are offered at 10:30am Monday to Saturday (with an extra 12:30pm tour on game days) between April and September. In other months there's a 10:30am tour on Monday, Wednesday and Friday. (☎215-463-1000; www.mlb. com/phillies/ballpark; 1 Citizens Bank Way, South Philadelphia; tickets from $20; Ⓢ AT&T)

### Lincoln Financial Field

STADIUM

26 ⭐ MAP P122, F6

The proud home of the Philadelphia Eagles (www.philadelphiaea gles.com) and occasional stage for mega-concerts. Since their Super Bowl win it's sure to be even more difficult to secure tickets to a game here. Even if you are lucky enough to score a seat it will not be cheap.

Pray for good weather as the stadium is notorious for tunneling the wind. Tours of the stadium are also available – book online. (☎215-463-5500; www.lincolnfinancial field.com; 1 Lincoln Financial Field Way, South Philadelphia; stadium tours adult/child $10/8; Ⓢ AT&T)

### Wells Fargo Center

SPECTATOR SPORT

27 ⭐ MAP P122, F6

Home of the National Hockey League team Philadelphia Flyers, the NBA Philadelphia 76ers, and the Philadelphia Soul of the Arena Football League. It's also a popular venue for concerts by major rock and pop artists.

Tours of the venue ($14) are available – check online for dates. (www.wellsfargocenterphilly.com; 3601 S Broad St, South Philadelphia; tickets from $23; Ⓢ AT&T)

### Theatre of the Living Arts

LIVE MUSIC

28 ⭐ MAP P122, G1

A century ago this venue was a nickelodeon and you can still see its roots as an old-time movie theater from its tiered levels of seating. Today it's used for music gigs and other performances organised through the promoter Live Nation. (TLA; ☏ 215-922-1011; http://venue.tlaphilly.com; 334 South St, Queen Village; 🚌 40, 57)

### Boot & Saddle

LIVE MUSIC

29 ⭐ MAP P122, B3

The iconic neon sign has glowed above the entrance to this bar for decades, but it's only in the last couple of years that the Boot & Saddle has reinvented itself as a great venue for live music, covering everything from indie rock and electronic to country. Shows are in the backroom and generally kick off around 7:30pm. (☏ 267-639-4528; www.bootandsaddlephilly.com; 1131 S

Lincoln Financial Field

FRANK ROMEO/SHUTTERSTOCK ©

South Philadelphia Entertainment

Broad St, Hawthorne; tickets from $15;
⏰ bar & restaurant 5-11:30pm Tue-Sun;
Ⓢ Ellsworth-Federal)

### South Street Cinema CINEMA

30 ⭐ MAP P122, G1

There are just 40 seats, a screen and a projector at this low-tech movie house, which screens cult, classic and indie movies. Theme nights include horror on Saturdays, B-Movie Thursdays, kids matinees on Saturdays and comedy flicks on Sundays (when there's live stand-up before the movie). (www.facebook.com/south streetcinema/; 327 South St, Queen Village; tickets $5; 🚌 40, 57)

# Shopping

### Eye's Gallery ARTS & CRAFTS

31 🔒 MAP P122, G1

Julia and Isaiah Zagar set up this gallery specializing in folk art, fashion and jewelry in 1968 as a place to sell Isaiah's work along with that of fellow traveler-artists. The products on sale here, many of which are created by artisans in places such as Peru, Mexico and India, add a brilliant burst of color and creativity to South St. (☎ 215-925-0193; www. eyesgallery.com; 402 South St, Queen Village; ⏰ 11am-7pm Mon-Thu, to 8pm Fri & Sat, noon-7pm Sun; 🚌 40, 57)

### Little Moon + Arrow TOYS

32 🔒 MAP P122, G2

We doubt you'll find a more adorable selection of handmade toys and kids' clothing – all made from organic materials – in Philadelphia. Choose between wooden toys by Grimms from Germany, the colorful animal creations of So Heart Felt and calming tinctures of Mothercraft, among other items. (☎ 267-457-5403; www.littlemoonand arrow.com; 729 S 4th St, Queen Village; ⏰ 11am-7pm Tue-Sat, to 5pm Sun; 🚌 40, 57)

### Philly Typewriter VINTAGE

33 🔒 MAP P122, D5

Are you suffering digital burnout? The solution lies at this store that stocks refurbished vintage typewriters, manual and electric. Genial co-owner Bryan Kravitz and his staff will happily extol the virtues of these analogue keyboards, which are displayed like museum pieces and start at around $275. (☎ 267-992-3230; www.phillytypewrit er.com; 1439 E Passyunk Ave, Passyunk Sq; ⏰ 10am-6pm Tue-Thu & Sat, to 7pm Fri; 🚌 45, 47, Ⓢ Ellsworth-Federal)

### Philadelphia AIDS Thrift FASHION & ACCESSORIES

34 🔒 MAP P122, F2

Arguably the mother of all Philly thrift stores, if you can't find a bargain piece of clothing or discover some fabulous fashion item here, you're not really trying. There's also plenty of books and household items for sale – and all the proceeds go to local groups involved in the fight against HIV/AIDS. (☎ 215-922-3186; http:// phillyaidsthrift.com; 710 S 5th St, Queen

Village; ⏱11am-8pm Mon-Thu, to 9pm Fri & Sat, to 7pm Sun; 🚇40, 57)

## Moon + Arrow
FASHION & ACCESSORIES

35 🔒 MAP P122, G2

As well as selling its own jewelry line, this wonderful boutique sells a broad range of handmade and vintage goods to wear and for the home. It's a big supporter of local brands and also host a variety of craft-related events. (📞267-457-5403; http://moonandarrow.com; 729 S 4th St, Queen Village; ⏱11am-7pm Tue-Sat, to 5pm Sun; 🚇40, 57)

## Molly's Books & Records
BOOKS

36 🔒 MAP P122, E3

Molly's offers an excellent selection of secondhand books and records, many of them quite rare finds. This being the Italian Market, there's a large section devoted to retro and modern cookbooks and food. (📞215-923-3367; www.mollysbooksandrecords.com; 1010 S 9th St, Bella Vista; ⏱10am-6pm; 🚇47, 🅂Ellsworth-Federal)

## Good's Vintage
VINTAGE

37 🔒 MAP P122, E3

Tucked away in the Italian Market is this quirky and attractive store that stocks all kinds of attractive vintage items. Specialties include silver and gold jewelry and small pieces of furniture, as well as a few clothes and decorative buys. (📞267-639-4744; www.etsy.com/shop/shopgoodsvintage; 1022 S 9th St, Bella Vista; ⏱10am-6pm Tue-Sat; 🚇47, 🅂Ellsworth-Federal)

Pat's King of Steaks (p130)

# Explore ◈

# University City & West Philadelphia

*Immediately west across the Schuylkill River from downtown Philly is the area that's home to both Drexel University and the Ivy League University of Pennsylvania (U Penn). The latter's leafy campus makes for a pleasant afternoon stroll and has an excellent museum and library. Further west, toward Spruce Hill, are the green spaces of Woodlands cemetery, Clark Park and Bartram's Garden.*

*U Penn, founded by Benjamin Franklin in 1740, dominates the neighborhood. You'll need no more than a day to tour around this area's key sights, the best of which is Penn Museum (p141). The exhibitions at the Institute of Contemporary Art (p139) rarely disappoint and it's certainly worthwhile wandering around U Penn's campus to admire the architecture and public art. Drop by 30th St Station (p139) to marvel at one of the grandest rail stations in the US, also swing by Bartram's Garden (p145), the oldest botanical garden in the US.*

## Getting There & Around

🚍 SEPTA buses crisscross the area and two LUCY bus services shuttle in a loop around University City.

Ⓢ Market-Frankford Line subway and trolley stations include 30th & 34th Sts. Trolleys also stop at 30th St and 33rd before lines split into north and south branches.

🚍 SEPTA Regional Rail lines and Amtrak long-distance trains arrive and depart from 30th St Station. Unversity City is also a Regional Rail station on the line that heads out the airport.

### Neighborhood Map on p140

# Walking Tour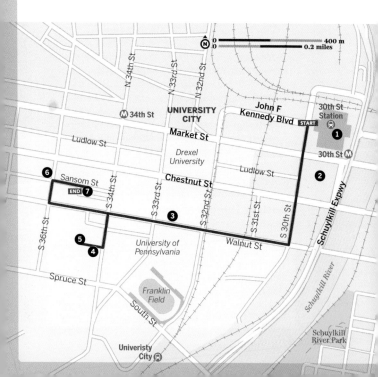

## Exploring University City

*Home to the campuses of several universities, the area immediately west of the Schuylkill River is the academic center of the city. It is also a place in which to admire a broad range of architectural styles, from Gothic Revival to contemporary, and creative pieces of art.*

### Walk Facts

**Start** S 30th St Station

**End** White Dog Cafe; S 34th Station

**Length** 1.5 miles; two hours

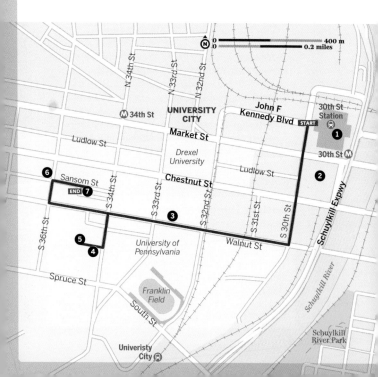

### ❶ 30th St Station

While taking in the grandness of **30th St Station** (30th & Market Sts; ⏱24hr; Ⓢ30th St, 🚆30th St) check out the *Pennyslvania Railroad WWII Memorial*, a giant bronze winged figure also known as the Angel of Resurrection, at the east end of the concourse. In a room off the concourse's north side is Karl Bitter's sculptural frieze *Spirit of Transportation*.

### ❷ Cira Green

Head to the roof of the parking garage for the Cira Centre South complex to find this grassy 1.25-acre **park** (www.ciragreen.com; 129 S 30th St; ⏱6am-10pm May-Sep, 7am-8pm Oct-Apr; Ⓢ30th St, 🚆30th St). It's a pleasant spot to relax and offers splendid views of the Schuylkill River and city skyline.

### ❸ Krishna P Singh Center for Nanotechnology

These striking 2013 interlocking glass **buildings** (3205 Walnut St; 🚌21, 42, 🚆University City) are set at angles and include a dramatic cantilevered box hanging three stories over the grassy courtyard in which you'll find Tony Smith's painted steel sculpture *We Lost*.

### ❹ Anne & Jerome Fisher Fine Arts Library

U Penn's magnificent 1891 **library** (📞215-898-8325; www.library.upenn.edu/finearts; 220 S 34th St; ⏱10am-5pm Mon-Fri; 🚌30, 42, 🚆37th St)

was designed by architect Frank Furness. The catalog and reading room, lit by clerestory windows and skylights and sporting a baronial fireplace, is one of the most beautiful you will ever see.

### ❺ Blanche P Levy Park

This small **park** (The Green; off 34th & Walnut Sts; 🚌30, 42, trolley 37th St) is dotted with public art including a *LOVE* sculpture by Robert Indiana. Local wags like to say that when the 1899 bronze of *Benjamin Franklin* sat down, a button from his vest popped off to created the giant white *Split Button*, a 1981 work by Claes Oldenburg.

### ❻ Institute of Contemporary Art

Andy Warhol had his first solo show **here** (ICA; 📞215-898-7108; www.icaphila.org; 118 S 36th St; admission free; ⏱11am-8pm Wed, to 6pm Thu & Fri, to 5pm Sat & Sun; 🚌21, 42, Ⓢ34th St) in 1965. There are usually two shows at any one time, but check the schedule, as there are periods when nothing is on between installations.

### ❼ White Dog Cafe

Drop in **here** (📞215-386-9224; www.whitedog.com; 3420 Sansom St; dinner mains $18-29; ⏱11:30am-9:30pm Mon-Fri, 10am-10pm Sat, 10am-9pm Sun; 🚌30, 42, Ⓢ34th St) to admire this farm-to-table restaurant's quirky collection of canine-themed art. Wine and cocktails go for just $5 during happy hour (4pm to 7pm weekdays).

University City & West Philadelphia

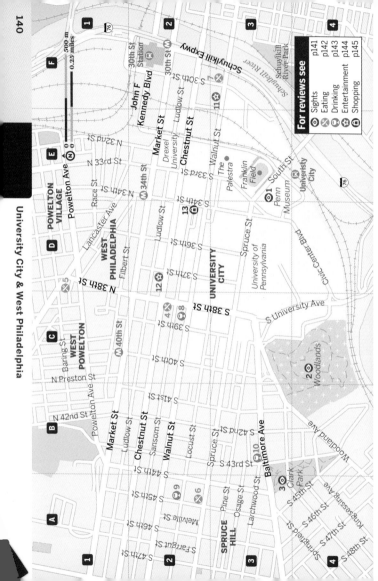

500 m
0.25 miles

**For reviews see**
| | | |
|---|---|---|
| ◎ | Sights | p141 |
| ✕ | Eating | p142 |
| ◐ | Drinking | p143 |
| ✦ | Entertainment | p144 |
| 🛍 | Shopping | p145 |

POWELTON VILLAGE

WEST PHILADELPHIA

WEST POWELTON

UNIVERSITY CITY

SPRUCE HILL

Woodlands

Clark Park

30th St Station

Schuylkill River Park

Schuylkill River

University City

Penn Museum

Franklin Field

The Palestra

University of Pennsylvania

30th St Expwy
Schuylkill Expwy

# Sights

## Penn Museum
MUSEUM

1 MAP P140, E3

U Penn's magical museum, the largest of its type in the US, contains archaeological treasures from ancient Egypt, Mesopotamia, the Mayan world and more. In April 2018 its new Middle East galleries opened, part of an ongoing transformation of the institution that will see various parts of it under wraps until around 2020.

Before taking in the museum's impressive galleries, take a moment or two to admire the building's eclectic 19th-century architecture and design, which includes a Japanese gate, arts-and-crafts brickwork, a rotunda, public gardens, sculptures by Alexander Stirling Calder and a koi pond. The Stoner Courtyard is the location for a series of outdoor summer **concerts** (⏰5-8pm Wed mid-Jun–early Sep). (☏215-898-4000; www.penn.museum; 3260 South St, University City; adult/child $15/10; ⏰10am-5pm Tue-Sun, to 8pm first Wed; 🚌21, 30, 40, Ⓜ36th St Station)

## Woodlands
CEMETERY

2 MAP P140, C4

This National Historic Landmark is a 54-acre cemetery that was once the country seat of William Hamilton, who hailed from a family of wealthy colonial lawyers and politicians. Two of Hamilton's 18th-century buildings stand in the grounds surrounded by

University City & West Philadelphia Sights

Penn Museum

## Food Trucks 🍽️

Several excellent food trucks do good trade around the university campuses and the southern side of 30th St Station. If they're not around, inside the station itself you'll also find a good food court.

elaborate Victorian funerary monuments and the shady trees he planted as part of his desire to craft an ideal English landscape. (☎215-386-2181; http://woodlands phila.org; 4000 Woodland Ave; tours $10; ⏲cemetery dawn-dusk; Hamilton Mansion tours 10am, noon & 2pm Thu Apr-Oct)

### Clark Park                    PARK

3 ◉ MAP P140, A3

Established in 1895, this 9-acre park is named after the former landowner Clarence H Clark, who was the first president of the First National Bank of Philadelphia. Near the park's Baltimore Ave end is the 1890 statue of *Dickens & Little Nell* by Francis Edwin Elwell. Public statues of the author are very rare as Dickens' will stipulated that there be no monuments or memorials of him.

A fantastic **farmers' market** (http://thefoodtrust.org/farmers-mar kets/market/clark-park) is held here every Saturday from 10am to 2pm

year-round, and on Thursdays from 2pm until 7pm in the summer. (www.friendsofclarkpark.org; 4300-4398 Baltimore Ave, Spruce Hill; ⏲24hr; 🚇Baltimore Ave & 43rd St)

# Eating

### Koreana                    KOREAN $

4 🍴 MAP P140, C2

Satisfying students and others interested in good, inexpensive Korean fare; enter from the parking lot in the back of the shopping plaza. The chicken wings are recommended, and it also does noodles, rice dishes and spicy stews. (☎215-222-2240; www.koreanafood. com; 3801 Chestnut St, University City; mains $8-11; ⏲11am-10pm Tue-Sun; Ⓢ40th St)

### Eat Café                    INTERNATIONAL $$

5 🍴 MAP P140, D1

The vibe is very relaxed and the food hearty and generally healthy at this community cafe, which is run on a non-profit, pay-what-you-can-afford basis. There are prices on the menu but they're suggestions. There's always several vegan options, with traditional brunch items served on Sunday. (☎267-292-2768; www.eatcafe.org; 3820 Lancaster Ave, West Powelton; mains $15-17; ⏲4:30-8pm Wed-Fri, 11am-2pm Sun; 🛜; 🚇Lancaster Ave & 38th St)

## The Farmacy
BREAKFAST $$

6  MAP P140, A2

If you're feverish for brunch, the Farmacy provides the cure in a variety of tried and tested ways. You can build your own eggs Benedict or get a guaranteed sugar rush from its s'mores french toast. Most social are the shareable boards of cheese and charcuterie paired with homemade jams and pickles. (☎215-387-3276; www.thefarmacyrx.com; 4443 Spruce St, Spruce Hill; brunch items $14; ⏱10am-2pm Thu & Fri, 9am-2pm Sat & Sun; ☒21, 42)

## Walnut Street Cafe
AMERICAN $$$

7  MAP P140, F3

Sitting at the base of the FMC Tower, this is a power dining spot with easy-on-the-eye decor and a generally play-it-safe menu of pasta, salads, burgers and steaks. It is a classy spot for breakfast (the pastries are among the best items) or brunch, which comes with jazz on Sunday. (☎215-867-8067; www.walnutstreetcafe.com; 2929 Walnut St, University City; mains $15-29;

⏱7am-9pm Mon-Thu, to 10pm Fri, 10am-10pm Sat, to 9pm Sun; ☒21, 42, 9, Ⓢ30th St)

# Drinking

## City Tap House
CRAFT BEER

8 🍺 MAP P140, C2

You can get very merry working your way through the 60 beers on tap here. This, as well as the outdoor terrace spread over two levels and decent food, make City Tap House the area's best bar by some distance. (☎215-662-0105; www.ucity.citytap.com; The Radian, 3925 Walnut St, University City; ⏱11:30am-midnight Mon-Fri, from 11am Sat & Sun; ☒40, ☒37th St)

## Fiume
BAR

9 🍺 MAP P140, A2

This unmarked dive bar, in a small room above the Ethiopian restaurant Abyssinia, has live music, great cocktails and a good selection of craft beers. It's cash only. Beware that it can be packed on weekends, when you might

---

### Sports Meets

Catch a basketball game in the hallowed halls of the **Palestra** (Map p140, E3; ☎215-898-6151; www.pennathletics.com; 223 S 33rd St, University City; ☒30, 42, ☒University City) or varsity football and track meets at **Franklin Field** (Map p140, E3; ☎215-898-6151; www.facilities.upenn.edu/maps/locations/franklin-field; 235 S 33rd St, University City; ☒30, 42, ☒University City).

find yourself stuck with your drink in the stairwell. (☎215-352-3591; fiumebar@gmail.com; 229 S 45th St, Spruce Hill; ◷6pm-2am; ☒21, 42)

## Green Line Cafe

CAFE

10 🜂 MAP P140, B3

This popular cafe is named after the trolley line that passes outside. It's a wonderfully relaxed spot to linger over an organic drip coffee, loose-leaf tea or a vegan soup. You can also get a takeaway to enjoy across the road in the green confines of Clark Park. (☎215-222-3431; www.greenlinecafe. com; 4239 Baltimore Ave, Spruce Hill; ◷6:30am-9:30pm Mon-Fri, 7am-9pm Sat, 8am-9pm Sun; ☒Baltimore Ave & 34th St)

# Entertainment

## World Cafe Live

LIVE MUSIC

11 🜂 MAP P140, F3

Home to U Penn's radio station, WXPN, this former factory is one of Philly's premier live-music venues. There are upstairs and downstairs performance spaces for jazz, folk and global acts, plus good food. (☎215-222-1400; www. worldcafelive.com; 3025 Walnut St, University City; cover $10-40; ◷from 11am Fri, from 5pm Sat-Thu; ☒21, 42, Ⓢ30th St)

## Lightbox Film Center

CINEMA

12 🜂 MAP P140, D2

On a mission to screen films that others don't – from classics

Franklin Field (p143)

SINITAR/SHUTTERSTOCK ©

## Exploring Bartram's Garden

North America's oldest botanic **garden** (215-729-5281; http://bartramsgarden.org; 5400 Lindbergh Blvd, Kingsessing; tour adult/student $12/10; 10am-4pm Mon-Fri, to 6pm Sat & Sun; Lindbergh Blvd & 54th St) dates back to 1728 when it was founded by Quaker farmer John Bartram. This lovely 45-acre National Historic Landmark, which includes the sturdy stone Bartram Hall and the Sankofa Community Farm, is open year-round with tours running Thursday through Sunday, from April 1 to December 3. Garden tours are at 1pm and 3pm and house tours at noon and 2pm.

Among other activities and events held here, there's free kayaking and rowing on Saturday between 11am and 3pm from end of April to the end of October. When the Schuylkill River Trail (https://schuylkillrivertrail.com) is completed in 2019, it will be possible to cycle, walk, and jog directly from Center City to the garden.

and forgotten gems to the most obscure of documentaries and art-house pics – the Lightbox provides a uniquely cinematic view on the world. Various festivals and retrospectives are held here and there are $5 matinees for families on Saturday. (215-387-5125; www.lightboxfilmcenter.org; International House Philadelphia, 3701 Chestnut St, University City; tickets adults/students $10/8; 21, 42, S 34th St)

# Shopping

### Penn Book Center BOOKS

13 MAP P140, D2

In its fifth decade, this friendly indie bookstore is not just a store, but a community worth seeking out and supporting. There's a good selection of local authors and knowledgeable staff. (215-222-7600; www.pennbookcenter.com; 130 S 34th St, University City; 10am-6pm Mon-Sat; 21, 30, 42, S 34th St)

# Survival Guide

Philadelphia from the Benjamin Franklin Bridge (p43) ALLARD ONE/SHUTTERSTOCK ©

# Before You Go

## Book Your Stay

o Philadelphia is compact, so it's generally not much of an issue which area you choose to be based. Most hotels, including plenty of national chains, are in the busy business district of Center City.

o Reservations are recommended for busy times of the year: major public holidays (especially Independence Day) and around graduation time for the universities and colleges.

o Taxes on accommodation are high. As well as the 7% hotel occupancy tax there's an 8% total sales tax and 8.5% hotel room rental tax.

o Hotel websites often include deals and package rates.

## Useful Websites

**A Bed and Breakfast Connection** (https://bnbphiladelphia.com) Reservation service

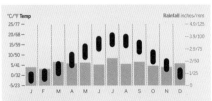

## When to Go

o **Winter (Dec–Feb)** Sub-zero temperatures, but the holiday season brings some sparkle. A perfect time for museum-hopping and there's also the Mummers Parade.

o **Spring (Mar–May)** Sunshine without the heat and crowds of high summer.

o **Summer (Jun–Aug)** The city is oppressively hot in the height of summer.

o **Fall (Sep–Nov)** Fall colors are painted across Philadelphia's parks. September is a great time to visit, particularly during the city-wide Fringe Festival.

for vetted B&B accommodations in the Philadelphia area.

**Philly Overnight Hotel Package** (www.visitphilly.com/features/visit-philly-overnight-hotel-package) Great package deals on stays of two nights or more with a variety of extras.

**Lonely Planet** (www.lonelyplanet.com/usa/philadelphia/hotels) Accommodation reviews and online booking service.

## Best Budget

**Apple Hostels** (www.applehostels.com) A friendly, well-managed hostel in the heart of Old City.

**Chamounix Mansion Hostel** (www.philahostel.org) An antique house amid Fairmount Park.

**City House Hostel: Old City Philadelphia** (www.cityhousehostels.com/philadelphia/old-city-philadelphia-hostel) Fun, pop-art decorated hostel in an old brick house.

**City House Hostel: Philadelphia House** (www.cityhousehostels.com/philadelphia/philadelphia-hostel) Offers a free beer and arranges pub crawls.

## Best Midrange

**AKA University City** (www.stayaka.com) Sleek interiors, fine amenities and wonderful city views.

**Study at University City** (www.thestudyatuniversitycity.com) Contemporary design darling amid the uni campuses.

**Thomas Bond House B&B** (www.thomasbondhousebandb.com) An 18th-century gem with no two rooms alike.

**Aloft Philadelphia Downtown** (www.aloftphiladelphiadowntown.com) Offers a youthful, stylish vibe and lofty rooms.

**Alexander Inn** (www.alexanderinn.com) Friendly and atmospheric with vintage style.

## Best Top End

**Hotel Palomar** (www.hotelpalomar-philadelphia.com) Lounge around in a leopard-print bathrobe at this stylish bolt-hole.

**Logan Philadelphia** (http://curiocollection3.hilton.com) Top digs, steps from some of the city's top tourist attractions.

**Rittenhouse Hotel** (www.rittenhousehotel.com) Great facilities and a fine location overlooking Rittenhouse Sq.

**Wm Mulherin's Sons** (http://wmmulherinssons.com) Four super-stylish rooms in trendy Fishtown.

# Arriving in Philadelphia

## Philadelphia International Airport

**Philadelphia International Airport** (PHL; ☎ 215-937-6937; www.phl.org; 8000 Essington Ave, Southwest Philadelphia; ⬛ Airport Line) is 10 miles southwest of Center City.

**Train** SEPTA's Regional Rail service connects the airport to the city. Trains run regularly between 5am and midnight, take around 30 minutes and cost $6.75

to Center City stations ($9.25 to other stations).

**Taxi** From the airport to Center City taxis charge a fixed flat rate of $28.50 for the first person, plus $1 for each additional person.

**Bus** SEPTA buses 37 and 108 serve the airport.

## Greyhound Terminal

Greyhound (www.greyhound.com), Peter Pan Bus Lines (www.peterpanbus.com), NJ Transit (www.njtransit.com) and the no-frills Chinatown Bus (www.chinatown-bus.org) all depart from the **Greyhound Terminal** (☎ 215-931-4075; 1001 Filbert St, Chinatown; ⬛ 11th St, ⬛ Jefferson) downtown, near the convention center.

## 30th St Station

Beautiful neoclassical **30th St Station** (☎ 1800-872-7245; www.amtrak.com; 2955 Market St, University City; ⬛ 30th St) is a major hub for train services.

From just west of 30th St Station,

**Megabus** (http://us.megabus.com; JFK Blvd & N 30th St, University City; **S**30th St, **R**30th St) serves major US cities in the northeast and Toronto. For NYC and Boston, **Bolt Bus** (☎877-265-8287; www.boltbus.com; JFK Blvd & N 30th St, University City; **S**30th St, **R**30th St) has the roomiest buses.

# Getting Around

## Bicycle

○ The bike-share system **Indego** (☎844-446-3346; www.rideindego.com) has stations located around the city. You'll need a US-registered credit or debit card to rent the bikes for the walk-up rate of $4 for 30 minutes.

○ Order an Indego key ahead of time. The IndegoFlex ($10 per year) gives you a rate of $4 per hour. The Indego30 ($15 per month) is the best deal if you plan to use the bikes a lot, as the first hour of every trip is free, before the $4 per hour kicks in.

○ A couple of good online resources for planning your cycling route are **GoPhillyGo** (https://gophillygo.org) and **Circuit Trails** (http://circuittrails.org)

## Bus

Market St is the main artery – hop on buses here to cross the center, or go underground to take the trolley to University City.

Between the end of March and the end of December, the purple **PHLASH** (☎800-537-7676; https://ridephillyphlash.com; 1 ride $2, day pass $5; ⏰10am-6pm, end Mar-end Dec) bus makes a loop around major tourist sites; tickets can be bought for cash (exact change only) on the bus.

## Car & Motorcycle

○ Driving isn't recommended in central Philadelphia; the traffic is heavy, parking is difficult and expensive, and regulations are strictly enforced.

○ Nearly all downtown hotels will offer valet parking but rates can be as much as $50 a day.

## Subway & Trolley

**SEPTA** (☎215-580-7800; www.septa.org) runs two subway lines: **Broad Street Line** (orange on the transit map), and **Market-Frankford Line** (blue); this line is also referred to as the El because it's an elevated line outside of the downtown area.

There are also several **Trolley Lines** (green), running underground along Market St and out to 30th St and beyond, where they emerge above ground again.

## Taxi

Cabs, especially around Center City, are easy to hail. Uber and Lyft also operate here.

## Train

SEPTA **Regional Rail Lines** head out to suburban destinations such as Norristown (the line for Manayunk and Wissahickon) or Chestnut Hill East (the line for Germantown).

**PATCO** (Port Authority Transit Corporation; ☎856-772-6900; www.ridepatco.org; 1-way any Philadelphia station &

## Dos & Don'ts

○ Smoking is banned in city-owned parks and in most bars and many restaurants.

○ People tend to eat dinner early in Philadelphia.

Camden $1.40) runs frequent subway trains to Camden, New Jersey. Stations in Philadelphia are 15-16th St, 11th-12th St, 9th-10th St along Locust, and 8th St at Market St. Then it's a scenic ride across the Ben Franklin Bridge to Camden.

### Tickets & Passes

○ Cash fares on all SEPTA transportation are $2.50 with $1 extra for transfers.

○ Purchase the stored-value **Key Card** for discounted fares of $2 per journey.

○ The **One Day Convenience Pass** ($9) is valid for eight trips on bus, subway or trolley.

○ The one-day **Independence Pass** (individual/family $13/30) offers unlimited rides on all buses, rail and subways, including the Airport Line.

# Essential Information

## Business Hours

Opening hours can vary throughout the year, sometimes widely, with most museums and many restaurants having longer hours in the summer (late May through early September) or on weekends.

**Businesses** 9am to 5pm; occasionally closed or have limited hours on Sundays.

**Cafes** Typically open seven days a week for breakfast and lunch.

**Restaurants** Hours vary; often fine-dining spots are open for dinner service only, from about 5pm to 10pm. Many close on Sundays and Mondays.

## Discount Cards

**Philadelphia Pass** (www.philadelphiapass. com) This pass covers admission to over 30 attractions as well as discounts on other sights, tours, shops and restaurants. To get the most out of it, however, you'll need to be sightseeing at a fairly fast pace. The pass is available for one (adult/child $59/44), two (adult/child $79/59), three (adult/child $89/69) and five ($109/89) consecutive days.

**CityPASS** (www. citypass.com) A good deal for families, this pass (adult/child $55/35) lasts nine days and covers access to the Franklin Institute, One Liberty Observation Deck and either the zoo or the Adventure Aquarium over in Camden. You can hop between each of the sites and others on Big Bus Company open-top buses, which are also covered by the pass.

## Electricity

The US electric current is 110V to 115V, 60Hz AC. Outlets are made for flat two-prong plugs (which often have a third, rounded prong for grounding).

**Type A**
120V/60Hz

**Type B**
120V/60Hz

## Emergencies

Report police, medical and fire emergencies by dialing ☎911. Hotels frequently require an additional ☎9 to reach an outside line: dial ☎9, then wait for the dial tone, then ☎911.

## Money

### ATMs

ATMs are common.

### Credit Cards

Major credit cards are accepted at most hotels, restaurants and shops.

### Changing Money

Banks and money-changers, common in central Philadelphia, will give you US currency based on the current exchange rate.

## Public Holidays

Banks, schools, offices and most shops close on the following holidays:

**New Year's Day**
January 1

**Martin Luther King Jr Day** Third Monday in January

**Presidents' Day** Third Monday in February

**Emancipation Day**
April 16

**Memorial Day** Last Monday in May

**Independence Day**
July 4

**Labor Day** First Monday in September

**Columbus Day** Second Monday in October

**Veterans Day**
November 11

**Thanksgiving Day** Fourth Thursday in November

**Christmas Day**
December 25

## Safe Travel

Philadelphia has no more dangers than the average big American city.
o Homelessness is widespread, but people are rarely aggressive.

o Avoid walking alone in poorly-lit areas.

## Telephone

Phone numbers within the US consist of a three-digit area code followed by a seven-digit local number. In Philadelphia, you will always dial 10 numbers: 1 + the three-digit area code + the seven-digit number.

## Money Saving Tips

o A good way to get between major sights is on the PHLASH downtown loop bus (day pass $5).

o It pays to eat dinner early as many downtown restaurants often have happy-hour specials on food between 4pm and 7pm.

## Mobile Phones

International travelers can use local SIM cards in a smartphone provided it is unlocked. Alternatively, you can buy a cheap US phone and load it up with prepaid minutes.

## Toilets

Before setting out to explore the Independence National Historical Park note that most of the historic buildings do not have toilets; use the facilities at the Independence Visitor Center.

## Tourist Information

**Independence Visitor Center** (☎ 800-537-7676; www.phlvisitorcenter.com; ⏱ 8:30am-6pm Sep-May, 8:30am-7pm Jun-Aug; Ⓢ 5th St) Run by the city and the National Park Service, the center cov-

ers the Independence National Historical Park and all of the sights in Philadelphia.

The city tourism service has convenient branches at **City Hall** (☎ 267-514-4757; www.phlvisitorcenter.com; ⏱ 9am-5pm Mon-Fri, 11am-4pm occasional Sat; Ⓢ City Hall & 15th St), **Logan Sq** (☎ 267-514-4760; 200 N 18th St; ⏱ 9:30am-5:30pm Mon-Sat, to 5pm Sun May-Sep; 🚌 27, 32, 33) and **JFK Plaza** (☎ 215-683-0246; 1599 John F Kennedy Blvd; ⏱ 10am-5pm Mon-Sat; Ⓢ City Hall & 15th St).

## Travelers with Disablities

o Philadelphia offers standard United States access and accommodations in restaurants and hotels.

o Newer museums have been designed with accessibility in mind; however, some historic sites may have limited

access due to the need for historic preservation.

o Download Lonely Planet's free Accessible Travel guide from http://lptravel.to/Accessible Travel.

## Visas

For the updated list of countries included in the Visa Waiver Program and current requirements, see the **US Department of State** (http://travel.state.gov) website.

Citizens of VWP countries need to register with the **US Department of Homeland Security** (https://esta.cbp.dhs.gov/esta) three days before their visit. There is a $14 fee for registration application; when approved, the registration is valid for two years or until your passport expires, whichever comes first.

You must obtain a visa in your home country if you:

o do not currently hold a passport from a VWP country;

o are planning to stay longer than 90 days;

o are planning to work or study in the US.

# Behind the Scenes

## Send Us Your Feedback

We love to hear from travelers – your comments help make our books better. We read every word, and we guarantee that your feedback goes straight to the authors. Visit **lonelyplanet.com/contact** to submit your updates and suggestions.

Note: We may edit, reproduce and incorporate your comments in Lonely Planet products such as guidebooks, websites and digital products, so let us know if you don't want your comments reproduced or your name acknowledged. For a copy of our privacy policy visit lonelyplanet.com/privacy.

## Simon's Thanks

Many thanks to the following people who generously shared their time and knowledge about the city: Jerry Silverman, Lindsay Ryan, Tish Byrne, Mason Wray and Rajeev Shankar.

## Acknowledgements

Cover photograph: Downtown Society Hill, Philadelphia. Christian Hinkle/Alamy©

Photographs pp26–7 (clockwise from top left): f11photo/Shutterstock©, Darren LoPrinzi/Getty Images©, Jamegaw/Shutterstock©, Jon Lovette/Getty Images©

## This Book

This 1st edition of Lonely Planet's *Pocket Philadelphia* guidebook was researched and written by Simon Richmond. This guidebook was produced by the following:

**Destination Editor**
Trisha Ping

**Senior Product Editors**
Kate Mathews, Victoria Smith

**Product Editor** Ross Taylor

**Book Designer**
Virginia Moreno

**Senior Cartographers**
Corey Hutchison, Alison Lyall

**Assisting Editors** Katie Connolly, Lauren O'Connell

**Thanks to** Anne Mason, Martine Power, Kirsten Rawlings

# Index

See also separate subindexes for:

Eating p157
Drinking p158
Entertainment p159
Shopping p159



**Sights 000**
Map Pages **000**

Sights 000
Map Pages **000**

**Sights 000**
Map Pages **000**

# Our Writer

### Simon Richmond

Journalist and photographer Simon Richmond has specialised as a travel writer since the early 1990s. He's long since stopped counting the number of guidebooks he's researched and written for Lonely Planet, but countries covered include Australia, China, India, Iran, Japan, Korea, Malaysia, Mongolia, Myanmar (Burma), Russia, Singapore, South Africa, Turkey and the USA. His travel features have been published in newspapers and magazines around the world, including in the UK's *Independent*, *Guardian*, *Times*, *Daily Telegraph* and *Royal Geographical Society Magazine*; and Australia's *Sydney Morning Herald* and *Australian* newspapers, and the *Australian Financial Review Magazine*.

**Published by Lonely Planet Global Limited**
CRN 554153
1st edition – December 2018
ISBN 978 1 78701 443 5
© Lonely Planet 2018 Photographs © as indicated 2018
10 9 8 7 6 5 4 3 2 1
Printed in Singapore